D0513360

The Embroidered Garden

Lois Vickers

PYRAMID BOOKS

For my mother, Marion

Editor **Eleanor Van Zandt**
Art Editor **Lisa Tai**
Special Photography **Clive Streeter**
Stylist **Melanie Ambrose**
Illustration **Doris Powell Technical Illustration**
Production Controller **Alyssum Ross**
Project Editor **Linda Burroughs**

This edition published in 1989 by Pyramid Books,
an imprint of the Octopus Publishing Group,
Michelin House, 81 Fulham Road, London SW3 6RB.

Text and Product design © Lois Vickers 1989
Book design and photography © The Octopus Group Limited 1989
ISBN 1 871307 73 2
Produced by Mandarin Offset – printed in Hong Kong.

Metric and imperial (standard) measurements
Measurements in this book are given first in metric and then, in parentheses, in imperial (standard) units. In many cases the equivalents have been rounded up or down for convenience; to convert 64cm to $25\frac{1}{4}$ inches, for example, simply makes the work unnecessarily complicated for those using inches; in this case 25 inches would be given. Therefore, either system can be used, but they *must not be mixed*: stick to one or the other throughout a project.

Acknowledgements
The publishers would like to thank the following for their kind permission to reproduce the photographs:
Heather Angel 27, 31, 47, 54, 63, 80, 124; Biofotos/Hazel le Rougetel 44; Boys Syndication/Jacqui Hurst 125; Eric Chrichton 82 above and below; Garden Picture Library/Brian Carter 81/Marijke Heuff 83/JS Sira 8; Steven Wooster 22; Perdereau-Thomas 53; Mary Evans Picture Library 9, 93, 94, 112, 113; Good Housekeeping Magazine/Peter Myers 12 below; Michael Holford 29; Insight Picture Library/Linda Burgess 10, 11, 28; NHPA/N A Callow 95; Octopus Publishing Group/George Wright 64 left and right, 65; Planet Earth/David Phillips 55.
Special Photography
Dudley Moss 12 above, 13, 45, 46, 51.
Clive Streeter 1, 2–3, 14–15, 16, 17, 18–19, 25, 32–3, 35, 36–7, 39, 40, 42–3, 56–7, 60, 61, 66–7, 68, 70, 73, 74–5, 77, 79, 85, 86, 87, 89, 90, 91, 96–7, 98–9, 100, 102–3, 104–5, 106, 107, 111, 114–5, 116, 119, 121, 123, 126–7, 131, 133, 137, 139, 141.

The publishers would like to thank the following for the loan of properties for photographs:
Laura Ashley lace cushions 57, blouse 119; Campion shawl 37; Clifton Nurseries bay tree 67; Gallery of Antique Costume and Textile hatbox 60, shawl, gloves, handbag and parasol 119; The Portobello Antique Stall blotter and pen 15, magnifying glass 127; Putnams bowl 137; Sarah Reynolds potpourri 137; Stanhope & Bowry suitcase 91, bottles and crocodile case 115; Tobias and the Angel chair and shawl 33, linen 40, towel rack 42, quilt 60, chair 67, quilt 75, basket 85, tray and cloth 97, quilt 115; Zebra pillows and quilt 97.

Thanks are due to Mrs Cara Ackerman at Dunlicraft Ltd, Pullman Road, Wigston, Leicester LE8 2DY, for arranging a supply of DMC threads, and to Campden Needlecraft Centre, High Street, Chipping Campden, Gloucestershire GL55 6AG, for their fast, efficient and very helpful mail order service.

Contents

$\mathcal{I}$NTRODUCTION

The idea behind this book linking embroidery and gardening germinated from my gradual realization that I could not think of one pursuit without using the terms of reference of the other. Both interests go back to childhood, and, as I grew up, I dabbled in one, then the other, at various times; but it was only when I took both up seriously that I realized how much the two activities enhance and reinforce each other.

As time went on, I met other embroiderers who were keen gardeners, and read about other gardeners who embroidered—notably the great English gardener Gertrude Jekyll (1843–1932). Since then, several books have been published on this theme, approaching it from academic, historical or practical viewpoints. I felt, however, that there was room for a book that treated the subject in a more personal way.

The book I envisaged would not only offer embroidered representations of garden subjects but also suggest that gardeners and embroiderers share the same motivation at practical and philosophical levels. I cherished the hope that I might encourage dedicated gardeners to take up the needle, and confirmed needleworkers to develop an interest in gardening.

For this reason I wanted this book to be practical, with detailed instructions for the embroidery projects and useful information about the plants. Copying is often frowned upon in artistic circles, but we all learn by doing, and we all get inspiration from other people's work. Gardeners are notorious for

'stealing' ideas (as well as cuttings if nobody is looking), but people usually adapt ideas and make them their own.

I know from my own experience that if someone is told exactly how to do something, she often goes on to find a better or a different way of doing it; whereas showing someone a finished result without showing her how it was achieved can result in all her energy being diverted into finding out how to copy it. A novice who wants to start a piece of embroidery, but who has neither the time nor the inclination to design an original project, may find that the experience of working within the secure limits of a project with instructions, or a kit, may bring the confidence to develop her own ideas.

My own progress as an embroiderer began with copying and proceeded through trial and error and many painful mistakes. At that time I could find few books dealing with the sort of representational work that interests me, and those I did find laid down rules which I seemed constantly to be breaking.

Similarly with gardening. Early on, I discovered from books that the correct way to furnish a garden with plants was to examine the site and then select plants accordingly. I must confess that I usually do just the opposite. I see a plant that I must have, buy it and take it home, or I buy a tempting packet of seeds and plant them. I look after the plant in its pot for a time, while I read all about it and decide what sort of home it would like. If I haven't got the conditions it needs, then I will set about creating them. Sometimes I throw out a plant that has not lived up to expectations. I have given up feeling guilty about my unorthodox approach, because in my medium-small garden, with average soil, it seems to work quite well.

For any gardener, colour and texture play a large part in the allure of plants, and pouring over the displays of fantasy in seed catalogues is a favourite winter occupation. I get the same thrill from gazing at colour charts for embroidery threads, and often a particular combination of shades can be the starting point for a design. Colour can also be a useful ally for the embroiderer when it comes to making blooms recognizable. The same simple daisy shape could represent a marigold when worked in bright orange; use royal blue and it would become a cornflower.

When considering plants for the garden or for embroidery, I am not merely interested in their appearance. I also like to take into account their history and their practical and medicinal uses, as well as any literary references I can find; botanical names can also be a good source of information about a plant's history.

This may be why many of the plants in my garden and in this book are cottage garden plants—they had to earn their place in the garden by offering more than just a pretty face. One particularly useful group of plants was once used to provide dyestuffs, and some knitters still like to grow and use these plants. I don't have time to dye my own threads, and I find that the huge range of colours available commercially is adequate for all my needs, so I don't grow dye plants. However, there are some other plants which, as an embroiderer, I like to have, for both practical and symbolic reasons.

Flax (*Linum usitatissimum*) is one of the most useful plants known to man. The seeds and oil provided by flax are used for a variety of purposes, but it is from the tough, fibrous stems that we get linen, a fabric especially prized by embroiderers. The flax plant also has very pretty blue flowers.

Saponaria officinalis is an old plant with pretty pale pink flowers, whose leaves and roots can be stewed to produce a soapy solution used for cleaning fabrics. It is sometimes still used for restoring ancient and delicate embroideries and tapestries. Lavender, too, has associations with washing—of fabrics as well as bodies—and is used for scenting linens and protecting woollen fabrics against moth attack.

All the other moth-repellent plants would also be on my list of embroiderers' plants. Almost by definition, an embroiderer will be interested in the qualities and characteristics of different textiles, and this usually means wardrobes and drawers full of fabrics made from natural fibres (rather than synthetic ones); and it's the natural fibres that need moth protection. What better plants for an embroiderer to grow than those which provide the motivation for small, useful embroidered items, as well as the plant material for filling them?

These scented articles represent just part of the wide range of projects covered in the book. The versatility of free-style embroidery and counted-thread work, both of which use different weights of fabric, gives them an advantage over the relatively stiff embroidery on canvas; they have many uses, from delicate items of clothing to more robust things such as cushions.

I hope that among the projects in this book you will find some that you wish to make—and, especially, that you will be inspired to create your own original embroidery designs on gardening themes.

Lois Vickers

THE FLOWER GARDEN

In a flower garden plants are grown not primarily for their foliage or their scent but for the beauty of their blooms. We choose them to complement and contrast with each other in terms of size, colour, texture and habit; and we position them with regard to their different times of flowering. We can extend our pleasure in them by cutting them to arrange indoors, or by drying them for the winter.

Flowers, whether growing in the garden or cut and arranged, are one of the most popular subjects for artists and photographers. For embroiderers, the added possibilities of depicting texture make flowers even more attractive. A single flower or a shrub in bloom can provide as much inspiration for the embroiderer as a colourful mixed bouquet or a whole flower bed.

Nevertheless, a variety and quantity of flowers, spanning a long season, will offer that much more inspiration. I always feel envious of owners of large gardens who can grow flowers in rows, as a crop for cutting, so that there are always plenty for the house without denuding the garden. Most of us don't have that much space. I try to make up for it by favouring flowers that have a long season if they are regularly cut, so that cutting them for arrangements keeps the plants blooming instead of stripping them bare.

Where space is short, annuals tend to get squeezed out, in favour of shrubs, bulbs and perennials. One solution is to extend the growing space with containers of various kinds. Many well-known annuals, such as pot marigolds and Shirley poppies, will thrive in containers. A less common annual which is really happy in pots is *Matricaria grandiflora*. It resembles a daisy, but without the petals, producing a continuous supply of golden balls on straight stems. You can cram a lot of plants into a pot without their becoming crowded, and if you keep cutting them, they keep coming. They look lovely with royal blue cornflowers or pale blue scabious. A potful of

Fuchsias are among the flowers most suited to realistic treatment in embroidery designs (see page 15).

Flowers offer a wealth of inspiration with an almost infinite variety of forms, sizes and colours.

them would make a good subject for a small embroidered picture.

Among the perennials that bloom over a long season, violas are a favourite, especially with embroiderers. Another good choice, which can also be accommodated as a single plant in a pot if there isn't room for a whole clump, is *Cheiranthus* 'Bowles' mauve'. This is a wallflower without the characteristic scent; its virtue lies in its persistent blooming and in its colours: the narrow leaves are the faded blue-green of old tapestries, and the purple flowers pale becomingly with age.

Dried flowers

In the winter, dried flowers can do a lot to brighten one's surroundings. If you have no garden, you can buy flowers already dried,

often in mixed bouquets, or you can buy fresh flowers and dry them yourself. As a student, trying to cheer up a dreary bedsitter, I would buy myself bunches of fresh statice, then dry them to prolong their decorative life.

The common name of statice, sea lavender, refers to its natural habitat, salt marshes, and to its usual colours, shades of purple and blue. However, it also comes in a variety of other colours, including pink and yellow, which go surprisingly well together. I have combined these colours in the wall pocket shown on page 25.

Now that I have my own garden, I enjoy growing statice myself for cutting and drying. If you want a mixture of colours, buy seed of mixed hybrids and grow them as half-hardy annuals. There are also perennials that make good garden plants, as well as being good for cutting. Both kinds need sun and good drainage.

A lesser-known member of the same family, *Statice suworowii*, is a perennial with long, thin pink flower spikes. It grows well in pots, and its twisted, dusty pink fingers have the texture of chenille yarn, which makes them a lovely subject for embroidery.

Designing with flowers

Like any other subject, flowers can be depicted in embroidery either realistically or in a stylized manner. For the wall pocket, I chose a stylized approach, isolating and simplifying the tiny individual calices that grow in clusters on the flower stalk.

By contrast, I chose to represent the grape hyacinth and the fuchsia on the greeting cards (see page 15) as faithfully as possible. If one chooses a flower for its significance (it might bear the name of the card's recipient – such as Rose or Heather, for example – or be associated with a special time of the year, such as an Easter lily), then it must be instantly recognizable.

The herbaceous border is the mainstay of many gardens, large and small. If it has been carefully planned, it can provide an eye-catching riot of colour from the beginning of spring to late autumn. Strong shapes and harmonious colours suit formal gardens, whereas a less rigid approach is better suited to cottage gardens. As a source of inspiration for embroidery designs it is invaluable, offering both individual specimens and groups and combinations of different species and varieties.

Falling somewhere between the random pattern made by the statice calices and the realistic grape hyacinth and fuchsia are the assorted blossoms depicted on the tie-back shown on page 19. Here I have selected a wide variety of blossoms, each of which, seen from above, has a simple circular shape. This repeating shape, as well as the white-on-white colour scheme, helps to give the design unity. The variety and individuality of the flowers is achieved by, first, observing and recording their dominant shapes and textures and then interpreting these aspects in suitable threads and stitches.

You can adapt this basic idea in all sorts of different ways, to suit different fabrics and colour schemes. To complement solid-coloured curtains, you could either use the curtain fabric itself and work all the embroidery in a contrasting colour or use a contrasting fabric with thread matching the curtains. Or you could devise your own design, choosing flowers of appropriate colours. When planning the design, bear in mind the relative sizes of your chosen flowers – in order to avoid, for example, heroic-sized daisies with diminutive peonies. Cut out paper circles of the appropriate sizes, then move them around on the full-size background until you get a pleasing arrangement. Then add the details that distinguish one flower from another, marking in petals and shaping the edges as appropriate.

A monochrome colour scheme allows you to play freely with shape, size and texture. If you prefer a realistic colour scheme – perhaps using a variety of bright-coloured flowers for a 'peasant-style' embroidery – you will need to colour the motifs before arranging them, so as to ensure a good balance.

If your curtain fabric is printed with a floral design, you could trace the motifs from it and use them as the raw material of the design. The use of whole motifs, arranged to fit the

shape, produces a more satisfying effect than if the fabric itself were used, with the inevitable cutting-through of motifs at the edges.

Another approach is to restrict yourself to one type of flower but use all the colours in which it occurs. Poppies, for example, come in a range of colours, both subtle and bright. You could even restrict the design to one flower, one size and one colour, and still get plenty of interest from the arrangement of overlapping circles.

This kind of flat pattern designing can, of course, be used to decorate many different kinds of object, such as cushions, lampshades and placemats.

Reference material for floral designs can be found in books of photographs or drawings and paintings. But there is nothing to equal the excitement generated by plants growing in your own garden. Even if you are not confident about drawing your own designs and prefer to trace flowers from a book, the real plant will give you valuable information about colour, texture and detail, as well as a feeling for the essential qualities of the flower that no photograph can provide.

As pretty as a picture . . . Flowers in containers – vases, flower pots and baskets – make splendid subjects for embroidered pictures. The prettily patterned basket in this photograph perfectly complements the crowd of forget-me-nots and has a textural quality admirably suited to interpretation in needlework.

FLOWER PICTURES

A single bouquet of flowers or a flowering plant makes an ideal subject for a small picture. It may not be a particularly original idea, but this doesn't matter; your own enjoyment of the colours and shapes will make it something special. To keep the project relatively simple, choose one type of flower, rather than a mixed bouquet, and work them in several shades of the same colour for the necessary contrast. Some flowers are easier than others; anything with a daisy form is easiest of all.

Plan your design on paper first, and transfer it to the fabric in a suitable way. Or, if you prefer to work more freely, sketch the positions of the flowers directly on the fabric using

a water-erasable pen. Whichever method you choose, pay careful attention to the shape and position of each flower. The individual blossoms of a bouquet or plant are like faces in a crowd: some will be looking straight at you, others will be in profile, some will have their backs towards you, some will be looking up or down. However, you need not portray the flowers realistically. If you prefer, you can stylize the arrangement, making all the flowers look straight out of the picture.

The setting for the flowers should usually be simple, to avoid detracting from them. It could even be perfectly plain, as in the case of the basket of dried flowers. A window makes an attractive and convincing background, since flowers and plants are often placed in front of a window to catch the sun. Although it's a familiar device, you can make it your own by faithfully depicting the details of the particular window. If you should move, the picture will be a surprisingly vivid reminder of your former home.

Embroidered pictures often look best if they are surrounded by a margin of fabric and perhaps a decorative border of some kind. When I embroidered the picture of the daffodils (an early effort), I made a number of

technical mistakes, one of which was allowing too little fabric around the edges, so that I was forced to cover them with a window mount. The finished picture had a rather cramped appearance. Years later, I re-framed this picture, stitching it to another, larger piece of fabric with machine satin stitch. This yellow border and the orange chain stitch border surrounding it echo the colours of the daffodils. The flowers now convey something of the exhilaration of early spring which originally inspired the picture.

It is obviously important for a picture of this kind to be truly rectangular. I created problems for myself when working the daffodil picture by using a small ring frame, which entailed moving the fabric around and thus distorting it. Before working a picture of your own, read the sections on 'Preparing fabric', 'Embroidery frames', 'Finishing methods' and 'Mounting and framing', on pages 139, 140–1, 141 and 142, respectively.

GRAPE HYACINTH & FUCHSIA GREETING CARDS

*Embroidered greeting cards are a pleasure to make as well as to receive. The grape hyacinth depicted on this card (*Muscari armeniacum 'Cantab'*) is shown when still in bud; only the lowest buds are on the verge of blooming, and the upper ones are still green. The delicate blooms of fuchsia* Magellanica molinae, *which are the palest imaginable shade of pink, are depicted in the other design. If you prefer, you could embroider the flowers in crimson and purple to suggest the more familiar fuchsia* Magellanica riccartonii.

Cards specially made for embroidery, with pre-cut windows, can be purchased in many art and craft shops. One of these was used for both the grape hyacinth card and for the fuchsia card also. They are available in a choice of colours. Whether you buy a special card or make your own, it is sensible to think about the colours of the flowers, the background fabric and the cardboard 'frame' so that they harmonize and complement the overall design. You may find it possible to buy the exact cards shown. If you use different cards, you will need to adjust the size of the design and the fabric accordingly. Or you can make your own card from a piece of stiff cardboard, following the measurements given, as described in steps 8 and 9. In this case, you can make the window and design any shape you like.

MATERIALS

Grape hyacinth greeting card
Piece of pale pink fine cotton or linen, 15 by 10.5cm (6 by 4¼ inches) – or, if you prefer to work on a frame, 25cm (10 inches) square
Piece of lightweight iron-on interfacing 15 by 10.5cm (6 by 4¼ inches)
DMC stranded cotton (floss), I skein each of the following colours: 3346, 3347, 3348, 798, 518, 597, 503, and 368
Fine crewel needle
Ring frame, 20cm (8 inches) in diameter (optional)
Thin tracing paper or tissue paper
Greeting card with window for embroidery (see above) OR piece of good quality stiff paper, 15 by 32cm (6 by 12⅝ inches)
Craft knife (optional)
Glue
Double-sided tape

Fuchsia greeting card
Piece of pale blue fine cotton or linen, 15 by 10.5cm (6 by 4¼ inches) – or, if you prefer to work on a frame, 25cm (10 inches) square
Piece of lightweight iron-on interfacing 15 by 10.5cm (6 by 4¼ inches)
DMC stranded cotton (floss), I skein each of the following colours: 819, 470, 471, 472 and 435
Fine crewel needle
Ring frame, 20cm (8 inches) in diameter (optional)
Tracing paper
Embroidery transfer pencil
Greeting card with window for embroidery (see above) OR piece of good-quality stiff paper, 15 by 32cm (6 by 12⅝ inches)
Craft knife (optional)
Double-sided tape
Glue

MAKING THE GRAPE HYACINTH CARD

1 Iron the interfacing onto the fabric (this stiffens the fabric so that you can work the embroidery in the hand; however, you can, instead, mount it in a ring frame (not too tautly, to avoid straining the bond between fabric and interfacing).

2 Trace the design. Position it on the fabric 2.5cm (1 inch) from the top edge and the same distance from each side. Tack (baste) it in place.

3 Working through the tracing, embroider the leaves and stem. Use a single strand of 3346 and stem stitch for the leaves. Use a single strand of 3347 and a wide stem stitch for the stem.

4 Work the buds in French knots, starting at the bottom and changing the colours and the sizes of the knots as follows: *row 1:* 3 strands of 798, thrice around needle; *row 2:* 2 strands of 518 and 2 of 798, twice around needle; *row 3:* 2 of 518 and 1 of 798, twice around needle; *row 4:* 2 of 518, twice around needle: *row 5:* 2 of 597 and 2 of 518, once around needle; *row 6:* 2 of 597, twice around needle; *row 7:* 3 of 503, once around needle; *row 8:* as row 7; *row 9:* 1 of 368, twice around needle; *row 10:* 1 of 3348,

◄ Embroidered greeting cards were once very popular and this charming custom is enjoying a revival. The grape hyacinth shown here makes a charming, spring-like and lasting memento of a special celebration.

► The fuchsia on this greeting card is an unusual very pale pink variety. Less showy than some of the more popular kinds (see page 8), its slender delicacy makes it the perfect flower for fine needlework.

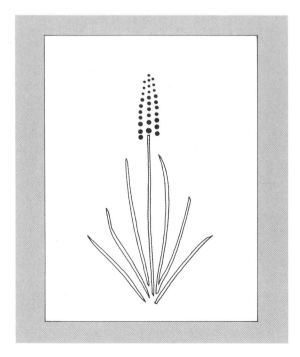

twice around needle.

In this case, it is best not to follow the tracing too precisely, so as to avoid too regular an appearance. If you pull the knots tightly, resulting in gaps, fill these in with extra knots.

5 Work the border, 2mm ($\frac{1}{8}$ inch) in from the outline, using 2 strands of 798 and running stitch.

6 Gently wash the work, if necessary (see page 141), and press it from the wrong side.

7 Attach the fabric to the centre section of the card with double-sided tape, then glue the right-hand section over the centre section, along the edges.

8 If you are making your own card: using a pencil and ruler, divide the piece of paper into three sections, measuring 10.6, 10.7 and 10.7cm ($4\frac{1}{8}$, $4\frac{3}{16}$ and $4\frac{3}{16}$ inches) in width. (The narrower section is the underside of the front of the card.) On the centre

3 Outline each part of the flowers and buds in split stitch, using a single strand of 819. Fill in with rows of split stitch, following the shapes of the outlines. The smallest part of the opened flower is worked in satin stitch. For the stamens, work French knots (thread 4 times around the needle) and a single straight stitch.
4 Work the leaves in buttonhole stitch, using 1 strand of 470; the calices in satin stitch, using 1 strand of 472; the flower stems in stem stitch, using 1 strand of 471. For the woody parts of the stem (between each flower stem and the next pair of leaves), use a single strand of 435 and work in a wide stem stitch.
5 Gently wash the work, if necessary, and press it from the wrong side.
6 Insert the work in a purchased card as described in step 7 of the Grape Hyacinth Greeting Card.
7 If you are making your own card, measure and mark the paper as described in step 8 of Grape Hyacinth Card. Trace the circle again, cut it out and use it to mark a circle lightly in pencil on the centre section of the paper, positioning it as in step 2, above. Cut out the circle.
8 Complete the card as for a purchased card.

section, mark and cut out a window, the exact size of the embroidery design area, positioning it 2.5cm (1 inch) from the top and sides.
9 Fold the two side sections inward. Complete the card as described in step 7, above.

MAKING THE FUCHSIA CARD

1 Prepare the fabric as described on page 16.
2 Trace the design, using an embroidery transfer pencil for the design itself and an ordinary pen for the circle. Making sure that the pen line has dried (test it on the edge of the fabric), position the motif, reversed, on the fabric with the circle 2.2cm ($\frac{7}{8}$ inch) down from the top and with the same amount of space on each side. Iron the design to transfer it to the fabric. Mount the fabric in the frame, if using one.

FLORAL TIE-BACKS

A simple, inexpensive white curtain takes on a romantic air when draped in graceful folds with this flower-strewn tie-back. The creamy white of the fabric contrasts subtly with the pure white of the threads. If you prefer, you could make it in colours, using one of the suggestions given on page 11.

MAKING THE TIE-BACK

1 Prepare the fabric as appropriate (see page 139).
2 Trace the outline of the tie-back; cut out the pattern and lay it aside. Using the embroidery transfer pencil, trace the whole design (see Note accompanying the design) onto another sheet of paper. Using a hard pencil, make another tracing of

MATERIALS (for two tie-backs)
40cm ($\frac{1}{2}$ yard) of closely-woven, medium-weight cotton fabric, at least 92cm (36 inches) wide; calico (unbleached muslin) was used for the tie-back shown and was first bleached in the washing machine.
40cm ($\frac{1}{2}$ yard) of heavyweight iron-on interfacing, at least 92cm (36 inches) wide
A selection of white embroidery threads, 1 skein each; those used for the tie-back shown are: stranded cotton (floss), no.5 perlé cotton, coton à broder, soft (matte) embroidery cotton, shiny rayon thread, by Marlitt (perlé cotton could be used instead)
Medium-sized crewel needle
Packet of bias binding
15 cm (6 inches) of 1.2cm ($\frac{1}{2}$ inch) ribbon seam binding
Sewing thread
4 curtain rings, 2cm ($\frac{3}{4}$ inch) in diameter
Tracing paper
Embroidery transfer pencil
20cm ($\frac{1}{4}$ yard) of transfer or ordinary fusing web

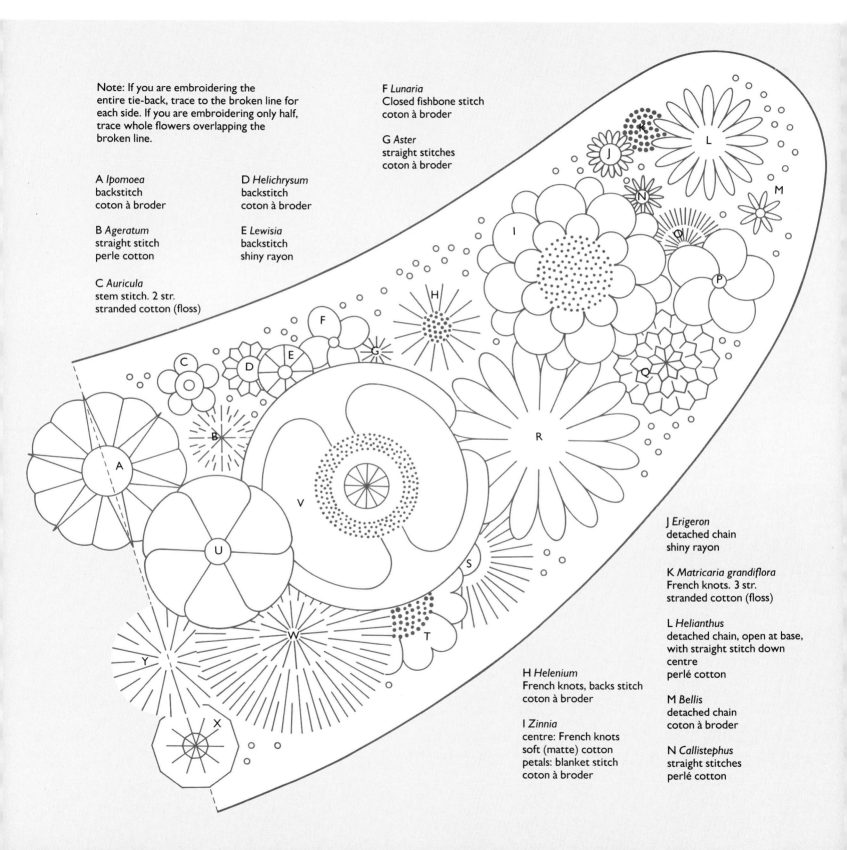

Note: If you are embroidering the
entire tie-back, trace to the broken line for
each side. If you are embroidering only half,
trace whole flowers overlapping the
broken line.

A *Ipomoea*
backstitch
coton à broder

B *Ageratum*
straight stitch
perle cotton

C *Auricula*
stem stitch. 2 str.
stranded cotton (floss)

D *Helichrysum*
backstitch
coton à broder

E *Lewisia*
backstitch
shiny rayon

F *Lunaria*
Closed fishbone stitch
coton à broder

G *Aster*
straight stitches
coton à broder

H *Helenium*
French knots, backs stitch
coton à broder

I *Zinnia*
centre: French knots
soft (matte) cotton
petals: blanket stitch
coton à broder

J *Erigeron*
detached chain
shiny rayon

K *Matricaria grandiflora*
French knots. 3 str.
stranded cotton (floss)

L *Helianthus*
detached chain, open at base,
with straight stitch down
centre
perlé cotton

M *Bellis*
detached chain
coton à broder

N *Callistephus*
straight stitches
perlé cotton

O *Gazania*
ring of open detached chain
filled with straight stitches;
alternate straight stitches
extend to centre
coton à broder

P *Linum narbonense*
curved lines of split stitch
following lines of petals
coton à broder

Q *Kerria*
fly stitches
coton à broder

R *Dimorphotheca*
closed herringbone stitch
coton à broder

S *Rudbeckia*
outer ring of buttonhole
stitch; inner ring of
buttonhole worked over ridge
of outer
coton à broder

T *Rosa*
2 rows of stem stitch,
French knots. 2 str.
stranded cotton (floss)

U *Ranunculus*
centre: buttonhole wheel and
French knots. 2 str.
stranded cotton (floss)
petals: blanket stitch. 2 str.
stranded cotton (floss)
threaded with I str. perlé cotton

V *Papaver*
centre: buttonhole wheel
coton à broder
stamens: French knots
perlé cotton
petals: blanket stitch
coton à broder

W *Chrysanthemum*
3 rows of detached chain
stitch with open ends
coton à broder

X *Kalmia*
stem stitch, straight stitch,
back stitch, French knots
coton à broder

Y *Calendula*
French knots
coton à broder
straight stitches
shiny rayon

◀ Trace the outline of the tie-back (actual size) for cutting out the fabric. Trace the entire design twice. Turn one of these tracings over and go over it with a transfer pencil to provide designs for both the left and right tie-back.

▼ Attach a curtain ring to each end of each tie-back with ribbon seam binding folded diagonally.
Inset   Attach bias binding to the underside of the tie-back, overlapping the ends as shown.

the design. Turn this over and go over the lines with the transfer pencil, so that you have designs for a right and left tie-back. If you plan to embroider the back of the tie-back as well, you will need to make two more tracings in the same way.
3 Using the plain pattern, and placing it on the fold, cut 4 shapes from the interfacing. Iron each shape to the wrong side of the fabric and cut around them.
4 Position the floral design tracings on two of these shapes and iron them off.
5 Following the instructions printed on the trace pattern, and using one strand of thread except where otherwise indicated, work the embroidery. (The interfacing makes the fabric stiff enough for the embroidery to be worked in the hand.)
6 When the design is complete, bond a plain tie-back shape to an embroidered one, using the fusing web. Trim any overlapping edges.
7 Using perlé cotton, work buttonhole stitch around each curtain ring.
8 Cut the seam binding into 4 equal pieces. Slip a curtain ring over one piece; fold the binding diagonally, as shown in the diagram below, and tack (baste) this loop to the edge of the underside of the tie-back as shown.

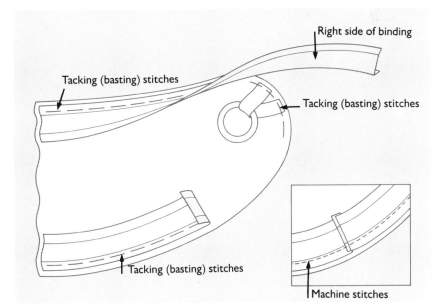

Right side of binding

Tacking (basting) stitches

Tacking (basting) stitches

Tacking (basting) stitches

Machine stitches

9 Unwrap the bias binding from the card, and tack (baste) it to the underside of the tie-back, starting at the plain end (which will face the window). When you reach the starting point, cut off the binding and overlap the ends as shown in the inset diagram on the previous page. Stitch the binding in place along the crease, by machine. Alternatively, you can stitch it by hand, using backstitch.

10 Turn the binding to the right side of the tie-back. Turn under the raw edge and stitch it in place, taking care to cover the first stitching, using either machine topstitching or slipstitch.

A curtain tie-back could also be embroidered in colour. It would probably be wise to restrict the design to a single type of flower, with a range of colours, to avoid a muddly and cluttered look. For example, the zinnias shown here display a wide variety of colours. The flower heads are the basic circle shape and added interest can be provided by thoughtful placing and overlapping.

STATICE WALL POCKET

The colourful little embroidered motifs decorating this wall pocket are based on the funnel-shaped calices of the statice, or sea lavender, plant. Use the pocket as a decorative container for holding bunches of dried statice or other dried flowers.

MAKING THE POCKET

1 Enlarge the design overleaf as instructed (see page 139). Trace the full-size outline of the pocket and cut it out. Use this pattern to cut 2 pieces from the interfacing.

2 Place the two interfacing pieces on the fabric, with side A aligned with the crosswise grain and with a little space around the shapes, and iron them in place. Cut out the shapes, adding 1.2cm ($\frac{1}{2}$ inch) around all edges.

3 Trace the enlarged design again, including the motifs and the two holes for piercing, using an embroidery transfer pencil. Iron it onto one of the fabric shapes (the other will serve as a lining).

4 Fold the edges over the interfacing on both pieces, and tack (baste) them in place. Set the sewing machine for a stitch length of about 3mm ($\frac{1}{8}$ inch). Machine stitch all around the outside of both pieces about 4mm (generous $\frac{1}{8}$ inch) from the edge. The colour of the thread does not matter. Remove the tacking (basting) stitches.

5 Using a single strand of perlé cotton, work blanket stitch along all edges of both pieces, working into the holes left by the machine stitching. Carefully cut and remove the machine stitching by pulling and unravelling.

6 Again using the perlé, and working into the existing holes, work stem stitch along the bottom of the blanket stitch on the front piece to form a horizontal ladder effect.

7 Using 3 strands of the floss, and following the colour placement shown on the pattern (or your own random placement), work the statice motifs as follows: bring the needle up at the neck of the funnel and work a single detached chain stitch along the right side, anchoring the stitch at the top right-hand corner; bring the needle up again, just inside the top of the loop, and work 6 buttonhole stitches to fill the shape, thus forming about one-quarter of a buttonhole wheel; anchor the last stitch, then work a straight stitch over the stem of the funnel.

8 Bond the plain and embroidered sections together using the fusing web (see page 138) and placing the embroidered side downwards.

9 Pierce the pocket at the two marked holes. Work buttonhole stitching around the holes, using the green perlé cotton.

10 Still using the perlé, oversew the two sections along all edges, working into the top of the blanket stitching.

11 Press the pocket again, with the embroidered side placed over a thick pad; while it is still warm, gently mould it into a cone shape.

12 Using strong sewing thread and making an extra-fat knot at the end, oversew the two short

MATERIALS

20cm ($\frac{1}{4}$ yard) of medium-weight, plain-woven green fabric

20cm ($\frac{1}{4}$ yard) of medium-weight or heavyweight iron-on interfacing

Piece of transfer or ordinary fusing web 18 by 37cm (7 by 15 inches)

Stranded cotton (floss), small amounts in colours shown: white, shell pink, salmon pink, lemon yellow, orange-yellow, blue-violet and magenta; actual colours used are DMC white, 3689, 352, 445, 982, 333 and 718, respectively

Stranded cotton (floss) in green to match fabric

No. 5 perlé cotton in green to match fabric

Medium-sized crewel needle

Tracing paper

Embroidery transfer pencil

1 metre (1 yard) of 3mm ($\frac{1}{8}$-inch)-wide satin ribbon to match one of the embroidery colours

Strong sewing thread in green to match fabric

Size: The completed wall pocket measures approximately 18cm (7 inches) in depth.

Enlarge the trace diagram below to twice the size. Trace the full-size outline and cut it out to make a pattern for cutting out the fabric and interfacing. Trace the full-size design again, including the motifs and marks for piercing, using an embroidery transfer pencil.

edges of the cone together, starting at the top. Leave the knot visible, so that when the pocket needs washing the final oversewing can easily be removed.
13 Thread the ribbon through the blanket stitches along the top edge, and tie it in a bow in front.
14 To fix the pocket to the wall, insert two drawing pins (thumbtacks) through the eyelet holes.

Note: Almost all flowers can be dried, but some are less inclined to lose their colour. Pick them in the morning after the dew has dried but before they are in full sun. Tie them loosely together in fairly small bunches with an elastic band (this will prevent the flowers from falling out if they shrink while drying). Hang them upside down in a cool, well-ventilated

place. Leave them until they are completely dry; the length of time this takes will vary depending on the type of flower, the atmosphere and the temperature. Very special or delicate blooms, such as early spring flowers or perfect roses, can be dried by laying them on silver sand, 'head to tail' without their petals touching and then gently covering them with a further thin layer of silver sand. A shoe box is an ideal container for this. This technique preserves the colours particularly well.

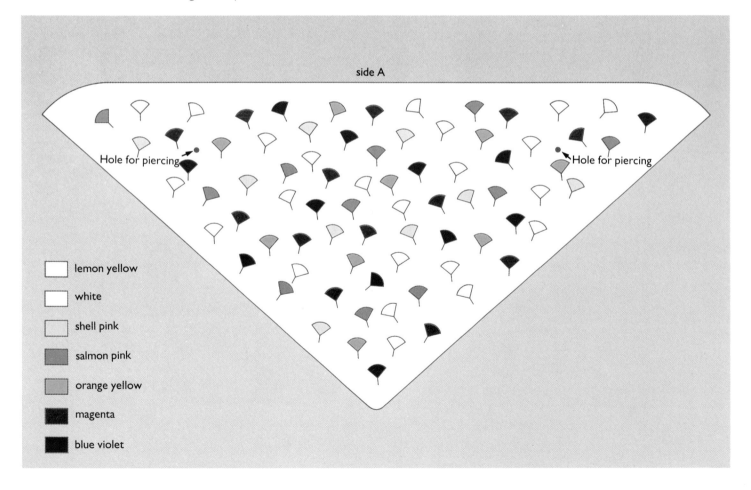

side A

Hole for piercing

Hole for piercing

lemon yellow

white

shell pink

salmon pink

orange yellow

magenta

blue violet

$\mathcal{T}$HE KNOT GARDEN

From its beginnings in Renaissance Italy, the fashion for rigidly formalized and symmetrically laid-out gardens quickly spread to other parts of Europe, including England; and during the sixteenth century this style of gardening became established as the most suitable for great houses. These gardens were like outdoor rooms, bordered with neatly clipped low hedges, whose floors consisted of geometrically shaped beds filled with flowers or differently coloured gravels. Unlike most modern gardens, they were not places in which to enjoy the different characteristics of a variety of flamboyant flowers and foliage, but an elegant setting in which lavishly apparelled ladies and gentlemen could be displayed to advantage, as if they themselves were gorgeous flowers.

The patterns of formal gardens echoed those of Oriental carpets. These precious objects were still a novelty in Europe (apart from Spain, where Muslim carpet weavers had lived and worked in the Middle Ages), and they were so prized that they were normally draped over tables rather than placed on the floor. The formal garden served as an outdoor counterpart (which *could* be walked upon, or through) to these luxurious textiles. Much later, the Victorians were to develop the idea further, with their brightly coloured 'carpet bedding', featuring exotic plants recently introduced from distant lands.

The sixteenth-century version was more restrained in colour, relying on a subtle contrast between the textures and different shades of green of the various types of foliage. In their design, however, they were highly elaborate. Those in France and Italy tended to be extensive and imposing, whereas in England they were designed on a more modest scale. There, they reflected the love of subtlety, intricacy and concealment characteristic of the Tudor court – traits that also appear in other decorative arts of the period, including plasterwork, woodcarving and embroidery.

The English knot
There were two distinct types of English knot garden (or simply 'knots', as the Elizabethans called them): open and closed. Both had closely clipped hedges of box or herbs, but open knots were simply scaled-down versions of the French and Italian originals, with the borders used as enclosures for flowers or gravel. Closed knots consisted almost entirely of strips of herbs, weaving over and under each other in complex intertwined patterns. Sometimes single bushes or clumps of plants were placed in the centre or in the loops formed by the design.

At the same time, mazes also became extremely popular. This type of garden strongly appealed to the Elizabethans, not only because of its complexity but also because of its symbolic value. The difficulties of

The Elizabethan knot garden at Cranborne Manor, Dorset, England is a fine example of a simple knot on a relatively restrained scale compared with more lavish Continental gardens.

the wanderer through the maze parallel the struggles of the soul to find its way through the twists and turns of life's fortunes.

Planning and planting

If you wish to create your own knot garden, you should give careful consideration to its siting and to the choice of plants. The garden should have full sun, if possible, and should be placed where it can be looked down on from an upstairs window or higher ground. Plants should be slow-growing; otherwise you will be forever clipping. Most of those suitable for knots grow best on a starvation diet; a rich soil means lush growth – to be avoided. You should also avoid the most complex designs, which require more labour than the private gardener can provide.

Box is a traditional favourite for knot gardens because it is evergreen and thickly leaved, so that it can be clipped close to the ground without looking sparse. Other plants favoured by the Elizabethans include lavender, hyssop, thyme, sage, rosemary, winter

Closed knots consist of complex intertwined patterns, as strips of herbs appear to wind over and under each other. The subtle variations in the shades of green and the differences in texture make such gardens an ideal direct source for embroidery designs.

Planting brightly coloured plants in the *parterres* was a later development in the history of the knot garden. This is a seventeenth-century design. They reached their most elaborate in the nineteenth century, with exotic colours and patterns that made the gardens resemble carpets and textiles.

savory, rue, marjoram and santolina.

Today, many different varieties of these plants are available, and you can have great fun planning a knot that follows the Elizabethan tradition and yet reflects your own preferences in colour, texture and scent. For example, there are many different thymes. Of the ordinary bushy green thymes, you can choose between thyme-scented and lemon-scented. There is an excellent form of common thyme called *Thymus nitidus* which is particularly resistant to winter die-back and has a very shapely habit, with narrower leaves than most. The golden variegated form 'Nyewoods' has a delicious lemon scent. Of the silver-leaved varieties, the thyme-scented

'Silver Posy' is a good choice, being relatively hardy. There are also various forms of creeping thyme, which could be used effectively as fillings within the hedges.

Among the varieties of rosemary, the common rosemary is probably the safest choice, although 'Tuscan Blue' is very tempting and grows thickly. Keep the plants pinched out right from the start, in order to prevent them from growing too tall.

The best marjoram is *Origanum onites* (pot marjoram), a spreading hardy perennial with neat leaves and pinkish flowers coming after lavender has bloomed. Another good choice is golden marjoram, *Origanum aureum*; in a sunny position its colour shows beautifully if it is kept well trimmed.

For santolina, choose a miniature one, *Santolina nana incana*. Winter savory, if cut well back when its pink flowers have faded, will stay neat for many years. It has the attraction of blooming rather later than most of the other plants.

Instead of the common sage, choose the narrow-leaved variety, which is more compact and has a better texture. Some of the variegated sages would be charming as little clumps in the middle of loops, though they are generally not robust enough to be used for the main part of the design.

Rue is ideal for knot gardens; it has a graceful habit and responds well to trimming. The lovely bluish-green leaves of Jackman's Blue are especially attractive.

Along with selecting the plants, the other major part of planning a knot garden is, of course, choosing or devising the design. You might use one of the designs interpreted here in embroidery; or, if you have the chance, look through old gardening books for a wider choice. Museums and historic houses may have plans and designs dating from the sixteenth and seventeenth centuries. You might even create your own original knot design.

You will first need to make a scale plan of the design. From this, you can calculate the number of plants you will need. Then divide the plan into squares, as for enlarging an embroidery design (see page 139). When you are ready to plant the garden, firm the soil by treading on it, or rolling it; then divide the area into squares, using pegs and twine (the same number of squares as on your plan). Transfer the design to the garden plot, square by square.

Embroidered knots

The designs for the embroidery projects in the following pages demonstrate the affinity between knot gardens and needlework. Indeed, it is likely that many of the designs given in Elizabethan garden books were adapted for embroideries of the time, and vice versa. Knot designs are especially well suited to cushions, because they are never upside down, whatever position they are in. And they are obviously ideal for herb sachets – the scent and the motif complementing each other.

You could easily create your own original knot garden embroidery, based on a design taken from a sixteenth-century pattern book or on that of a garden you have visited. If you wish to do a realistic interpretation of the knot, choose several shades of green thread to suggest different foliage. You could then enhance the colour contrast by using each shade for several different stitches to give the effect of different tones. Chain stitch, French knots, and buttonhole stitch, for example, provide a good contrast.

Or you might prefer to use the design as a starting point for a more stylized piece of stitchery, as was done for the ribbon and ball cushion on page 32. Once you start exploring the fascinating pathways of knot gardens, you will surely find them a rich source of inspiration.

This extraordinary garden in the Monasterio de San Lorenzo de Trassonto, Santiago de Compostela in North Spain is made from box clipped into allegorical designs. It has been maintained since the seventeenth century. A design like this could be converted into a spectacular quilted embroidered cushion.

RIBBON AND BALL CUSHION

Satiny, ribbon-like loops encircle the central ball motif of this cushion, which is based on an actual knot garden design in a seventeenth-century book.

1 Prepare both fabrics as appropriate (see page 139). Make sure that the weave of the main fabric is straight. From each fabric cut two pieces at least 50cm (20 inches) square. Neaten the edges of one square of linen and one of backing fabric. Set the other pieces aside.

2 Place the linen square on top of the backing square, aligning the edges carefully. Pin them together, then tack (baste) them together through the centre in both directions, following the weave of the top fabric.

3 Mount the fabric on a square frame (see page 140).

4 Enlarge Diagram A as instructed, and trace it 4 times on one sheet of paper, joining the tracings at the dotted lines to make the complete design.

5 Measure off 17.5cm (7 inches) from the centre point along one line of tacking. Mark this point, then work a line of tacking at right angles to it, following the weave of the fabric and working outwards 19.5cm (7¾ inches) to either side of the centre line. Repeat on the remaining three sides. These lines establish the inner edge of the border.

6 Place one of the tracings on top of the fabric. Pin it in place, aligning the centre and inner border lines, then tack (baste) it firmly through the centre in both directions.

Note: for successful results it is important to be very accurate in tracing, enlarging and transferring the lines of this design.

MATERIALS

50cm (⅝ yard) of pale green evenweave linen (see page 138) at least 100cm (40 inches) wide, with 25/26 threads to 2.5cm (1 inch)

50cm (⅝ yard) of soft white cotton or linen backing fabric, at least 100cm (40 inches) wide, to reinforce main fabric (optional)

DMC no. 5 perlé cotton in the following colours and quantities: 209 (2 skeins), 210 (5 skeins), 208 and 211 (1 skein each), and 744 (3 skeins)

DMC stranded cotton (floss) in the following colours: 208, 209, 210 and 211 (one skein each)

Medium-sized crewel or chenille needle

Medium-sized tapestry needle

Cushion pad (pillow form) 45cm (18 inches) square

35cm (14 inch) zip fastener

Tracing paper

Water-soluble pen or tailor's pencil

Ruler

Size of finished cushion: approximately 45cm (18 inches) square

WORKING THE EMBROIDERY

1 Using one strand of perlé cotton, shade 210, work the outlines of the looped ribbons in stem stitch. Keep the thread on the outside of the curve throughout, and always work in the same direction; avoid pulling the stitches too tightly. Where one loop goes under another, take the thread under the fabric and continue on the other side. Working directly over the tracing in this way helps to ensure a smooth outline.

2 Now fill in the ribbons with more lines of stem stitch. To ensure even spacing, mark each line with water-soluble pen (or tailor's pencil); mark the first line in the centre, then stitch along it; then mark two more between the centre line and the edges. Continue subdividing and stitching in this way until you have 17 rows of stem stitch lying side by side.

3 Mark in all the other design lines, except the diagonal yellow lines and French knots, using small tacking (basting) stitches (or, for utmost accuracy, backstitch).

4 The centre ball is embroidered in radiating rows

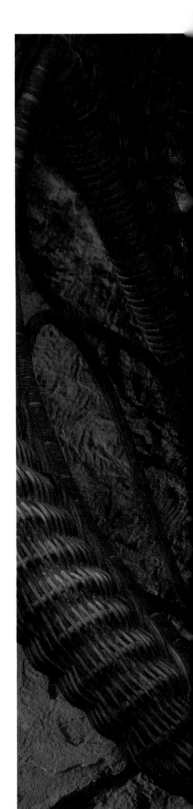

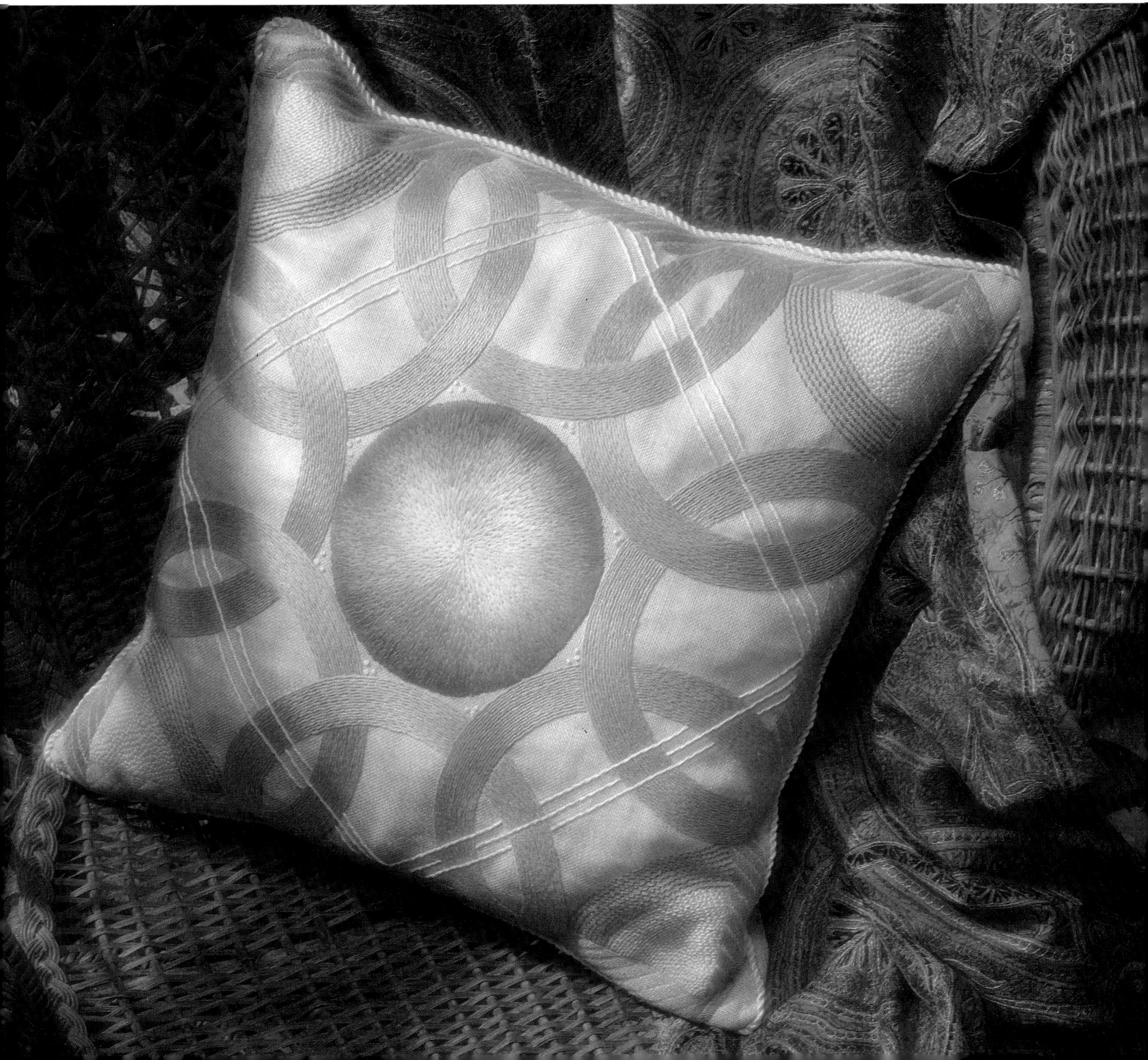

of long and short stitch, using 4 strands of floss in the needle. Begin by marking a series of concentric circles on the main motif. First mark a circle with a radius about one-third the larger radius. Then divide the outer circle into 6 rings of equal width. Use the colours as follows: centre circle, shade 211; ring 1, 210 and 211 (two strands each); ring 2, 210; ring 3, 209 and 210; ring 4, 209; ring 5, 208 and 209; ring 6, 208.

5 Now work the pattern-darned border, using one strand of perlé cotton, shade 209, and a tapestry needle. Begin at a right-hand corner, 23 fabric threads to the right of the line of tacking marking the adjacent border. Darn over 9 fabric threads and under 1, working across to the first ribbon loop.

Then work the next row, one thread down from the first, beginning one vertical thread to the left. Continue in this way until 23 rows have been darned, taking the last couple of rows across the whole width, up to the tacking for the next border. Fill in the remaining rows of the border, keeping the diagonal pattern correct. Repeat on the remaining three sides.

6 The corner quadrants are worked in concentric rows of backstitch. Mark and stitch the rows as for the ribbon loops, beginning at the edges and subdividing the sections with the marking pen. Use one strand of perlé cotton in 208 for the 9 rows of the outer section; one strand of 211 for the 30 rows of the inner section.

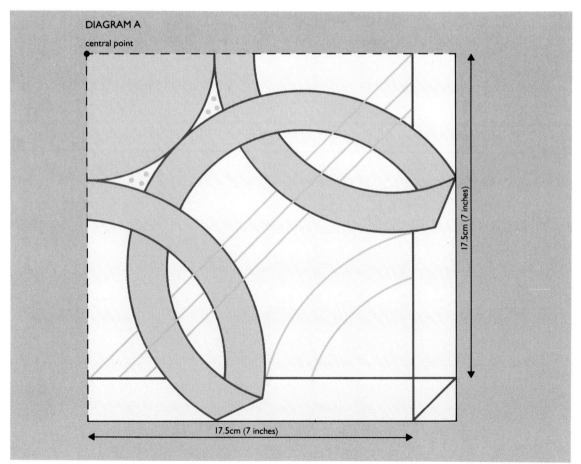

DIAGRAM A

central point

17.5cm (7 inches)

17.5cm (7 inches)

Before you can use **Diagram A** as a pattern for the cushion, you must enlarge it to twice the size given here, using the method described on page 139 (or a photocopying enlargement service). Then trace the full-size version 4 times onto the tracing paper, rotating it around the central point; do not reverse the design.

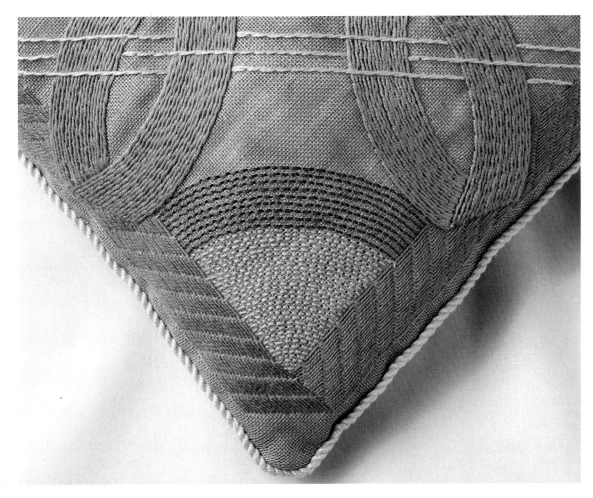

When the embroidery is complete, the cushion should be made up and trimmed with a twisted cord, a detail of which is shown here. This is made from 8 strands of perlé cotton, shade 744. Sew the cord around the edges of the cushion cover by hand.

7 Using the marking pen and a ruler, mark in the yellow lines, taking care to follow the printed design exactly. Embroider the lines in a single strand of perlé cotton, shade 744, using stem stitch and keeping the thread always on the same side of the needle. Using the same thread, work three French knots in the positions indicated on Diagram A (see opposite page).

MAKING UP THE CUSHION

(See the general comments on washing, pressing and blocking, page 141.)

1 Trim the fabric, leaving a margin of 3cm (1¼ inches) around the darned border on all sides. This includes a 2cm (¾ inch) seam allowance. Tack (baste) the other piece of backing fabric to the other linen square, through the centre and around the edges, and treat them as one layer.

2 Make up the cushion as described on page 141, inserting a zip in one side and leaving a small gap for the cord ends. Trim the seam allowances to different widths to reduce bulk.

3 Using two skeins of perlé cotton, shade 744, opened out and then folded into 8 even strands, make a twisted cord (see page 142). Hand-sew the cord around the edges of the cushion cover, overlapping and tucking the ends into the gap. Insert the cushion pad.

QUILTED CUSHION AND SACHET

The maze knot garden design used for this quilted cushion is complemented by similar designs used for the detachable sachet filled with soothing herbs.

PREPARATION

1 Prepare the fabric (see page 139). From the main fabric cut two pieces at least 48cm (19 inches) square. Cut a piece the same size from the backing fabric and from the wadding (batting).

2 Reinforce the edges of one piece of sateen, and mark the centre with lines of tacking (basting) (see page 32).

3 Mount this piece of fabric on a square frame (see page 140).

4 Enlarge Diagram B as instructed, and trace it onto a sheet of tracing paper, repeating it 4 times to make the complete design. Include the dotted lines, which will serve as a guide to placement.

MATERIALS

50cm (⅝ yard) of furnishing sateen, at least 115cm (45 inches) wide, in light green

50cm (⅝ yard) of lightweight cotton, any width, for backing

50cm (⅝ yard) of thin wadding (batting)

DMC no. 5 perlé cotton in the following colours and quantities: 819 and 3078 (3 skeins each for cushion only; one extra skein each for sachet)

DMC stranded cotton (floss) in the following colours: 819 and 3078 (one skein each, for sachet only)

Sewing thread or quilting thread to match fabric

Fine and medium-sized crewel or chenille needles

Needle for quilting (between or sharp)

Cushion pad (pillow form), 40cm (16 inches) square

Dried herbal sachet: a mixture of lemon verbena (*Lippia citriodora*) and eau-de-cologne mint (*Mentha citrata*) is good, as is woodruff (*Asperula odorata*). Choose something that will last a long time, and make sure that it is thoroughly dry.

30cm (12 inch) zip fastener

Tracing paper

Size of finished cushion: approximately 39cm (15½ inches) square; sachet: 12cm (4¾ inches) square

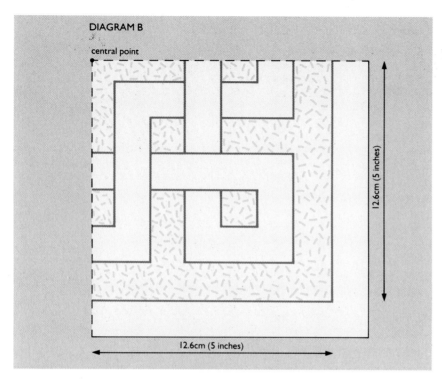

DIAGRAM B

central point

12.6cm (5 inches)

12.6cm (5 inches)

Diagram B gives one-quarter of the complete design for the cushion. It must first be enlarged to twice this size, using the method described on page 139. Then trace the full-size version 4 times onto tracing paper, rotating it around the central point: do not reverse the design.

5 Position the tracing on the fabric, aligning the dotted lines with the tacking, and pin it in place. Transfer the design lines with small tacking (basting) stitches. Carefully tear away the paper.

WORKING THE EMBROIDERY AND QUILTING

1 Thread two embroidery needles with a single strand of pale pink (819) and pale yellow (3078) perlé cotton. Work seeding stitches all over the background, mixing the colours randomly. The stitches should be about 3mm ($\frac{1}{8}$ inch) long.

2 Remove the fabric from the frame. Place it over the squares of wadding and backing, and tack (baste) the three layers together in both directions, starting at the centre and working outwards at about 5cm (2 inch) intervals, forming a grid. Take care that the fabric does not pucker. Re-frame the fabric.

3 Using a single strand of matching sewing or quilting thread, quilt along the design lines with a small running stitch (or backstitch, if you prefer a solid line). Pull out the original tacking stitches as

you go. When the quilting is complete, remove the tacking used to join the layers.

MAKING UP THE CUSHION

1 Trim the finished work, leaving a margin of 9cm ($3\frac{1}{2}$ inches) all around; this includes a 2cm ($\frac{3}{4}$ inch) seam allowance.

2 Make up the cushion as described on page 141, inserting a zip in one side and leaving a small gap for inserting the cord ends.

3 Make a twisted cord (see page 142), using one skein each of pale yellow and pale pink perlé cotton, each opened out and folded into 8 strands. Hand-sew the cord around the edges of the cover, making a loop about 13cm (5 inches) long at one corner, if a sachet will be added. Overlap the ends and tuck them into the gap. Make sure that the loop is sewn firmly in place. Insert the cushion pad.

MAKING THE SACHET – PREPARATION

1 From the remaining fabric cut two pieces, each at least 15cm (6 inches) square. On each piece mark the centre with two lines of tacking (basting). (Or mark only one piece, if you prefer to leave one side blank.) Oversew the edges.

2 Mount the fabric to be embroidered on a small frame.

3 Trace diagrams C and D (or just one of them) onto a piece of tracing paper. Pin and tack (baste) one of the tracings to the framed fabric, aligning the dotted lines with the centre tacking.

SACHET – WORKING THE EMBROIDERY

1 Using one strand of the floss, work the outlines of the interlaced pattern in split stitch, working through the tracing. (Use shade 3078 for design C, 819 for design D – or vice versa if you prefer.) Carefully pull the tracing away from the stitching. Use tweezers to remove any stubborn bits of paper.

2 Fill in the stitched outlines with more lines of split stitch, using the method described in step 2 of the Ribbon and Ball Cushion for accuracy.

3 Finally, work tiny seeding stitches (design C) or French knots (design D) in the shaded areas of the design, using the contrasting colour. Use 2 strands for the seeding, one for the French knots.

4 Mount the other piece of fabric in the frame, and work the other design, following steps 1–3.

MAKING UP THE SACHET

1 Trim each square evenly to measure 14cm (5½ inches); this includes a 1cm (⅜ inch) seam allowance. Tack (baste) and stitch them together, right sides facing, leaving a gap of about 5cm (2 inches) in one side so that the sachet can be turned. Turn the sachet right side out.

2 Using 8 strands of each shade of perlé cotton, make a twisted cord 65cm (25 inches) long (see page 142). Slipstitch it to the edges of the sachet, making a loop about 20cm (8 inches) long at one corner and leaving the ends loose across the gap. Make sure that the loop is firmly stitched at the corner.

3 Fill the sachet generously with the herb mixture. Close the gap with slipstitching, at the same time overlapping and inserting the cord ends (see page 38).

4 To attach the herb-filled sachet to the cushion, pass the sachet loop through the cushion loop, then pull the sachet back through its own loop. Do not pull too tight.

This side of the sachet shows the completed design for which the trace diagram – D – is given below right. The completed design on the other side, for which the trace diagram is C, is shown in the photograph on page 37.

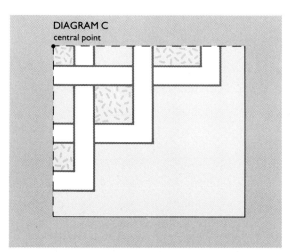

DIAGRAM C
central point

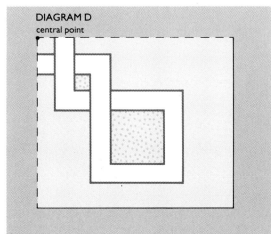

DIAGRAM D
central point

Diagram C, for one side of the sachet, is given full-size, but it needs to be traced 4 times to make the complete design. When tracing, rotate the paper around the central point.

Diagram D, used for the other side of the sachet, is also given full-size. Trace it 4 times to obtain the complete design, rotating the paper around the central point. Either of these designs could be used for a cushion if suitably enlarged (see page 139).

MOTH-REPELLENT SACHETS

A selection of herbs, all highly effective against moths, have been used as fillings for these two sachets. The counted-thread design represents a herb garden of wormwood (centre), rue (squares) and rosemary (corners). The curved design is based on hedges of cotton lavender surrounding beds of pinks.

MATERIALS

Herb garden sachet

Piece of mint green hardanger fabric with 22 paired threads to 2.5cm (1 inch), at least 24 by 12cm (9½ by 5 inches)

DMC stranded cotton (floss) in the following colours: 368, 562 and 3345; also a shade to match fabric (one skein each)

Dried herbal sachet, such as a mixture of equal parts wormwood (*Artemisia absinthium*), rue (*Ruta graveolens*) and rosemary (*Rosmarinus officinalis*) for filling

Small tapestry needle

Finished size of herb garden sachet: 10cm (4 inches) square

Hedge design sachet

Piece of bluish green hardanger fabric with 22 paired threads to 2.5cm (1 inch), at least 30 by 15cm (12 by 6 inches)

DMC stranded cotton (floss) in the following colours: 369, 3685, 3687, 3688 and 3689; also a shade to match fabric (one skein each)

Dried herbal sachet, such as southernwood (*Artemisia abrotanum*), for filling

2 small pearl buttons or beads

Small crewel needle

Small tapestry needle

Tracing paper

Finished size of hedge design sachet: 12.5cm (5 inches) square

DIAGRAM E

| | DMC 368 | | DMC 562 | | DMC 3345 |

MAKING THE HERB GARDEN SACHET

1 Cut the fabric into two squares, then trim each square to measure 92 (paired) threads across. On each square turn under 3 threads on each side, and sew them in place with small running stitches, using a single strand of the matching floss. Then, using the same thread, go over the edges with oversewing stitches, including the raw edges. These lines of stitching will be concealed by buttonholing. Mark the vertical and horizontal centres of the square with tacking (basting), sewing between two pairs of threads.

2 Thread the tapestry needle with 2 strands of shade 562. Starting 3 threads in from the edge, work buttonhole stitch around all four edges of one square; leave 2 fabric threads between the stitches.

3 Following the chart (Diagram E), work the embroidery, using 2 strands of thread and the colours and stitches indicated.

4 If a loop for hanging is desired, make one from 8 strands of shade 562 (see page 142). Sew this to one edge of the back square.

5 Buttonhole stitch the edges of the back square as described in step 2.

6 Place the two squares together with wrong sides facing. Join them with running stitch, using 2 strands of shade 562, along the base of the buttonholing, working over and under 2 fabric threads and leaving a small gap for stuffing.

7 Fill the sachet with the herbs; then complete the line of running stitch.

8 Finally, secure the edges by oversewing along the top of the buttonholing, again using 2 strands of 562.

MAKING THE HEDGE DESIGN SACHET

Note: The hardanger fabric used for these sachets is stiff enough so that a small piece of embroidery can be worked in the hand.

1 Cut the fabric into two squares, then trim each square to measure 116 (paired) threads across.

Diagram E represents one-quarter of the herb garden sachet. Each line of the grid represents 1 fabric thread. The central cross is worked in double cross stitch, the corners, in large Algerian eye (not pulled tight). The other areas of the design are worked in ordinary cross stitch.

Neaten the edges as described in step I of 'Herb Garden Sachet', and mark the centre of one square with tacking (basting).

2 Buttonhole around the edge of the square to be embroidered, as described in step 2 of 'Herb Garden Sachet', using shade 369.

3 Trace Diagram F 4 times onto tracing paper, joining the tracings along the dotted lines.

4 Tack (baste) the tracing over the square to be embroidered, centring it over the tacking.

5 Using 2 strands of 369 (in a crewel needle) and split stitch, work the outlines of the hedges through the tracing. Pull away the paper. Add another line of split stitch to fill in the hedge outlines.

6 Fill in the flower beds with French knots, using 2 strands of thread and placing the different shades of pink as shown in the diagram.

7 Make a cord for hanging (if desired) and complete the sachet as described in steps 4–8 of 'Herb Garden Sachet'; but add a second line of running stitch to the first, to make a solid line (Holbein stitch).

8 Sew the two buttons or beads to the centre to suggest a pond or garden ornament.

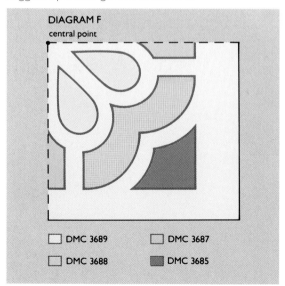

DIAGRAM F

central point

☐ DMC 3689   ☐ DMC 3687
☐ DMC 3688   ▨ DMC 3685

Diagram F shows one-quarter of the hedge design sachet, full-size. It is not necessary to pivot this design when tracing it, because it is symmetrical. Join the quarters along the dotted lines to make the complete design.

GUEST TOWEL

The colourful design on this green guest towel was inspired by formal beds of wallflowers planted in a municipal park. It is worked in a combination of darning stitches and French knots, which complement the pile of the towelling.

WORKING THE EMBROIDERY

1 Count the horizontal threads in the border of the towel, and work a line of tacking (basting) along the centre thread (actually a group of threads). Also mark the vertical thread.

MATERIALS

Guest towel designed for embroidery in grass
  green, measuring 25.5cm (10 inches)
  across
DMC no. 5 perlé cotton in the following colours:
  347, 703, 743, 745 and 3328 (one skein each)
Soft (matte) embroidery cotton in a shade to
  match the towel
Stranded cotton (floss) to match the towel
Medium-sized tapestry needle

2 Following the chart (Diagram G) and starting at the centre of the motif, work the design in French knots and darning stitches. Use a single strand of thread in the tapestry needle. Each French knot is worked diagonally over one thread intersection, from lower left to upper right.

3 Secure the fringe at each end of the guest towel with a row of buttonhole stitch, using a single strand of matching cotton floss and working from the wrong side of the fabric.

Diagram G shows one half of the design for the guest towel. Each line of the chart represents one fabric thread.

The thicker lines represent darning stitches; the dots, French knots. The colour key is below.

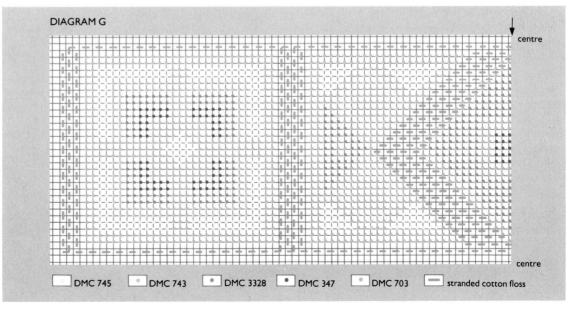

DIAGRAM G

centre

centre

| DMC 745 | DMC 743 | DMC 3328 | DMC 347 | DMC 703 | stranded cotton floss |

$\mathscr{I}$NTO THE GARDEN

Although gardening and embroidery may seem quite unconnected, they have traditional and historical links, as can be seen in the many beautiful embroideries depicting gardens and the countless interpretations of flowers in embroidery throughout the world. For me, as for many other people, the two interests have developed together.

The fascination of gardening, for some enthusiasts, is the opportunity it provides to create a world of one's own, or perhaps to recapture the lost world of one's childhood. Embroidery is in some ways the same, providing a haven in which to avoid for a while the stresses of life. Although both gardening and embroidery can be solitary pursuits, there are always fellow devotees who will generously share ideas and information.

The rose 'Madame Alfred Carrière'

Gardeners often use walls and hedges to enclose a space within a garden, with a gateway or archway offering a glimpse of a private place. The same device is useful for embroiderers, who can create, with the textures and colours at their disposal, the illusion of a framed view which draws the observer in.

This embroidered picture expresses some of my feelings about gardens. Scent is important in a garden, and lavender is, for me, indispensable. In my own garden I have no room for the luxury of a whole hedge, of either lavender or yew, but in an embroidered garden anything is possible. Similarly, to give one rose the run of a long wall is possible only in my dreams, but the rose in the picture (Madame Alfred Carrière) can have all the space it needs. This is a beautiful noisette rose with creamy-white flowers which are richly scented. It is useful for its particular hardiness and its ability to flower well even on a north-facing wall.

Work and rest

The wheelbarrow and the garden bench represent the two main joys of a garden – labour and rest. For any gardener these must be in balance. There can be little pleasure for the gardener when the amount of work to be done reproaches him, so that he cannot enjoy what he has made. In an embroidered garden, however, everything is always at its best. The grass will never need cutting, nor the hedge clipping. The path will not be spoilt by

weeds, and the lavender will always be ready for harvesting.

If it is properly cared for, lavender makes one of the best low hedges. It thrives best in very well drained, chalky soil, in full sun. Once the plants are established, the soil can scarcely be too dry or too poor. Regular hard trimming is essential. In mild areas you can do this after flowering; otherwise leave it until spring. If you treat your bushes like this, they will last longer and flower better. For this embroidered garden I chose a lavender with mauve blossoms (Hidcote or Twickle Purple), because they show up better than blue against the lawn.

I like to compare this picture with the more colourful one shown below, which I embroidered 11 years ago. It is always popular at exhibitions, and the flowers shown are based on real ones, but now that I have learned more about plants I know that the blooms would not have appeared simultaneously, as they do in the picture – something that irks me whenever I look at it!

Framing the view

The use of a framing device, such as a hedge with an opening, is a simple way to show depth in a garden picture without the use of complicated perspective – which is not generally appropriate in embroidery. Here, however, I have also used some perspective, in the arched opening of the hedge and the pathway, because I wanted the path to disappear enticingly, leaving a little to the imagination.

It is a good idea to keep an eye open for garden 'frames' as a basis for embroidery designs. There are all sorts of interesting gateways and arches, in brick, stone, wood and iron. Other framing devices include clipped hedges and trained climbing plants on trellises. The contrast between the foreground close up and the distant view can be enhanced by the choice of colours and types of thread and stitch. If you want to make a picture using fine thread and small detail, like this one, the frame approach is ideal, because it limits the amount of work by concentrating all the detail in the centre of the picture.

Although part of the charm of this detailed type of embroidery is its realism, it's a mistake to aim for photographic accuracy, which will certainly lead to disappointment. Instead, concentrate on suggesting different textures with appropriate stitches.

A collection of flowers like these, including sedum, hollyhock, aubretia, dianthus, polygonum, gypsophila, and lupin, would not be in bloom all at the same time in a real garden. However, it does not really matter too much and I am quite glad that I did not realize it at the time I embroidered them because it makes a lovely picture anyway. Planning the layout of a herbaceous border in shades of one colour as here, gives a muted and subtle result, but a variety of different complementary and harmonious colours could be mixed for a more dazzling virtuoso display

A view through a window can also be used as a framing device for creating an embroidered picture. Here, the surrounding darkness and the delicate geometric tracery of the metalwork contrast tellingly with the rich greenery seen beyond.

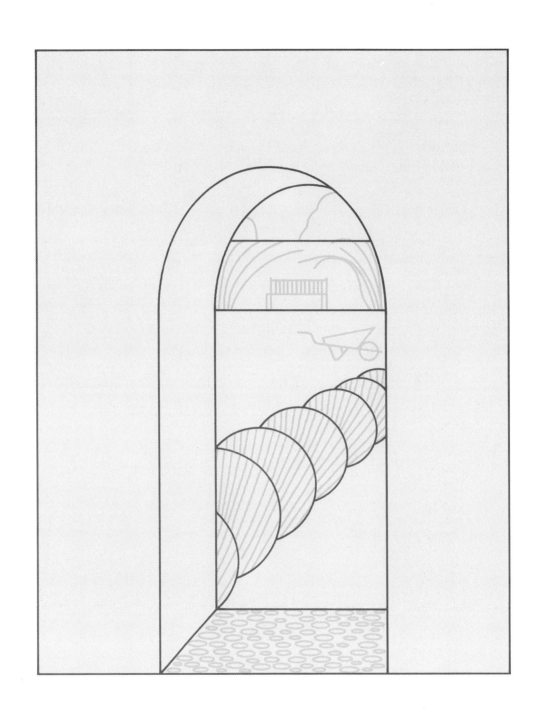

INSTRUCTIONS FOR WORKING THE PICTURE

Part of the pleasure of working this embroidered picture lies in the variety of stitches used to create different textures, and in the subtle gradations of colour.

In the trace pattern for the picture, the dark grey lines are the ones to be transferred to the fabric at the outset. The wheelbarrow, bench and climbing rose stems are traced separately and superimposed on the work later; the lines indicating the tree foliage, lavender stems and cobblestones may be traced if desired (see steps 2 and 3 of 'Preparing the fabric').

PREPARING THE FABRIC

1 Prepare the fabric as described on page 139.
2 Trace the main lines of the design, printed in dark grey, onto a sheet of tracing paper. At the same time, you may wish to trace the lines of the cobblestones and lavender stems, although these can be worked more freely if you prefer.
3 Trace the lines for the wheelbarrow, the bench and the stems of the climbing rose onto separate small pieces of tissue paper. You may also wish to trace the curved outlines of the foliage, to use as a guide when working the trees.
4 Transfer the main design onto the fabric, using dressmaker's carbon or the prick and pounce method (see page 140).
5 Using sky blue fabric paint, colour in the sky area. Test the paint on spare fabric first, and apply it very lightly, to obtain a delicate shade of blue. Allow this to dry.

6 Paint the hedge, applying the colour fairly thickly and taking care to stay inside the lines. Allow the paint to dry; then fix the colours by ironing with a warm iron on the wrong side.
7 Mount the fabric on the frame, as described on page 140.

WORKING THE EMBROIDERY

(Unless otherwise stated, the thread used is stranded cotton [floss].)
1 Begin the embroidery by working the cobblestones. First work the mossy background for the stones, by filling the whole area with closely worked rows of backstitches, each about 8mm ($\frac{3}{8}$ inch) long, using a single strand of DMC Medicis wool, shade 1410. The cobblestones themselves are the sort I have in my own garden. They are thin, flat stones from the river bank, laid on edge. You might want to change the colour or shape of the cobbles in your own picture. I used 2 strands of thread, and each cobblestone was made by working 3, 4 or 5 backstitches (each about 3–5mm [$\frac{1}{4}$–$\frac{1}{2}$ inch] long) side by side, using colours 317, 318, 646, 844, 3022 and 3041 randomly.
2 Now embroider the gravel path in French knots, in a variety of shades: 315, 318, 414, 640, 642, 644, 840, 841, 842, and a little white. Use 2 strands of thread, and graduate the sizes of the knots as described in the caption for the detail picture. Use more of the bolder colours at the front and paler ones at the back, mixing them in the middle.
3 Continue by working the brick wall. This is worked in darning stitches, staggering the stitches to suggest actual brickwork. (See the detail photograph on page 151.) I worked the stitches over a regular number of fabric threads (over 5 and under 1), but you can simply regulate them by eye, keeping them about 2mm ($\frac{1}{8}$ inch) long. Be sure to leave a fine line of fabric showing between the rows of stitches,

MATERIALS

Piece of good quality calico (unbleached muslin) or other heavy plain-woven cotton, 45 by 40cm (18 by 16 inches)
DMC stranded cotton (floss), 1 skein each of the following colours: 317, 318, 646, 844, 3022, 3041, 315, 414, 640, 642, 644, 840, 841, 842, 122, 368, 369, 500, 520, 700, 701, 702, 703, 772, 986, 987, 988, 989, 3348, 503, 504, 552, 553, 554, 3013, 3053, 3022, 3348, 712, 632; also white
DMC perlé cotton no. 5, 1 skein each of the following colours: 890, 904, 986, 987, 3345, 3346
DMC Medicis wool, 1 skein each of the following colours: 8409, 8410

Danish Flower Thread, 1 skein each of the following colours: 4, 14, 15, 27, 210, 218, 222, 235 (or other fine, matt-finish thread; see instructions for placement and colours)
Crewel needle, size 10 (or 9)
Fabric paint: sky blue and dark green
Paintbrush
Tracing paper and tissue paper
Piece of sturdy cardboard, 30 by 26cm (12 by 10 inches)
Strong thread for lacing
Dressmaker's carbon, or materials for prick and pounce transfer method (see page 140).
Size of finished picture: 20 by 16cm (8 by 6¼ inches, including fern stitch border.

to suggest mortar. I used a single strand of Danish Flower Thread for this. The main colour here is shade 15. To suggest the variation of colour characteristic of old brick walls, I left out a brick here and there (about 4 or 5 in each row), then filled in the gaps with colours 4, 14, 27, 218, and 235.

4 Next, work the lawn, using Cretan stitch (see diagram) and a single strand of thread. Work the stitches closely together, beginning at the top and working each row so that it encroaches on the one above it. Also vary the length of the stitches, from about 3mm ($\frac{1}{8}$ inch) at the top to about 8mm (nearly $\frac{3}{8}$ inch) at the bottom. I worked 17 rows to fill the space and used the following colours (from back to front): 772, 369, 3348, 368, 122 (the middle tone of this shaded thread), 989, 703, 988, 702, 987, 701, 987, 700, 986, 520, 986, 500. The stitches should encroach slightly into the area marked for the lavender.

5 The lavender stems are straight stitches, worked in a single strand of thread. Work from back to front, working each bush from left to right and then from right to left to form a crisscross effect. For all but the front two bushes use shade 504; for the next one use 503 for the first layer and 504 for the top; for the front bush use 503 for both layers.

6 The flower heads are worked in French knots, using 1 strand of thread. Use 554 at the back, 553 in the middle, and 552 at the front, blending the colours so that there are no sharp colour changes. Work from the back towards the front, gradually increasing the size and number of knots.

7 Tack (baste) the tracing of the bench to the work, then embroider it through the tissue, using straight stitches and a single strand of Danish Flower Thread, shade 222. See the detail photograph for its construction. Two straight stitches are used for the main lines of the bench, single stitches for the slats.

8 The trees behind the wall are worked in seeding, using a single strand of thread. (If you have traced the outline, tack [baste] it over the sky, and work through the tissue.) Those on the left are worked in shade 3013, those on the right in 3053. Work the stitches freely, as shown in the photograph, spacing them close together at the centre of the tree and thinly towards the edges. Tear away the tissue.

9 Tack (baste) the tracing of the climbing rose stems over the wall area. Then, using a single strand of shade 3022, work split stitch along the lines. When completed, carefully tear away the tissue.

10 Work the leaves of the climbing rose in seeding, using 2 strands of shade 3348 and placing them randomly. Then work the roses, also at random, in French knots, using a single strand of shade 712, wrapped once around the needle.

11 Tack (baste) the wheelbarrow tracing to the work, and embroider it as follows, using a single strand of thread throughout. For the wheel, work two circles of split stitch, in shade 646; work the body of the barrow in vertical satin stitch, then add a row of closely worked buttonhole stitch along the top edge, all in shade 646. Work straight, radiating stitches over the wheel, using 632, then work the remaining lines in split stitch in the same colour.

12 The hedge is embroidered in two layers. For the bottom layer, work horizontal, encroaching rows of Cretan stitch, using a single strand of Medicis wool

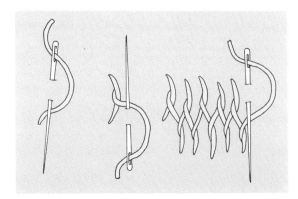

Cretan stitch can be worked in various ways. For the grass, the stitches should be worked in encroaching rows and placed close together, but they should not be too even. Those used for the under layer of the hedge are much longer, but are also placed close together in encroaching rows.

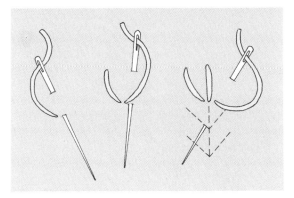

Fern stitch consists of three straight stitches converging on a central point. It is worked in lines, which can be straight, as shown here and in the border of the picture, or in curves, as for the sprigs in the yew hedge.

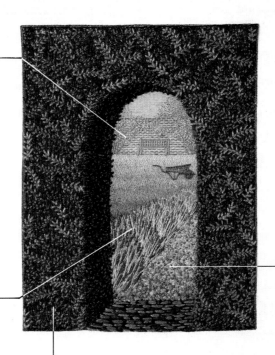

▲ (Step 3) This detail shows the colour variation in the brick wall. To achieve this, work most of the bricks in shade 15, leaving a gap here and there; fill in the gaps with the other colours.

▲ (Step 7) This photo shows the bench slightly enlarged; its actual size is shown on the trace pattern. Two straight stitches are used for the main lines, single stitches for the slats.

▼ (Step 2) The French knots for the path should be graduated by winding the thread 3 times around the needle for those in front, twice for those in the middle and once for those in the back. To flatten out the texture further, mix in some seeding (small straight stitches). Use more of the bolder colours at the front and paler ones at the back.

▲ (Step 5) Each lavender bush is worked in two layers: the first (marked on the trace pattern) from left to right, and the second, overlapping it, from right to left.

▲ (Step 6) For the distant bushes, work scattered French knots, wrapping the thread once. As you move forward, group them in lines of 3, 4, then 5 knots, and increase the size.

◀ The rich texture of the yew hedge is achieved with three layers: a foundation of fabric paint, a layer of Cretan stitch and freely curving lines of fern stitch, worked in several shades of perlé cotton. Begin with the arch, bringing some of the stitches over the edge to break it up. Then work the sprigs over the front of the hedge. Use the different shades of green randomly, taking care to avoid forming patterns.

and making the stitches about 2.5cm (1 inch) in the main section and 2cm ($\frac{3}{4}$ inch) deep within the arch; use shades 8409 and 8410 respectively. Stagger the stitches so that the rows encroach on each other slightly. The yew sprigs of the upper layer are worked in fern stitch (see diagram and the detail photograph above). Begin with the underside of the arch, working the stitches in a single strand of perlé cotton, shade 890. Work the main part of the arch in shades 904, 986, 987, 3345 and 3346.

13 Work the fern stitch border, using a single strand of Danish Flower Thread, shade 210, and making the stitches about 3mm ($\frac{1}{8}$ inch) long. Work in the same direction throughout, and extend the border by one stitch at each corner.

FINISHING
Remove the embroidery from the frame. Lace it over the piece of cardboard as shown on page 142. Frame it as desired.

CLIMBING PLANTS

CLIMBING PLANTS

Most plants, once settled in earth, will stay put and do as they are told, growing and developing in a fairly predictable way. Others, however, have a will of their own and like to wander. They may trail, run over the ground, or haul themselves up into the branches of their more sedate neighbours. These climbers and creepers work their own embroidery in the garden, by wreathing themselves around the supports provided or anything else they can reach. They make regular patterns or wild, abandoned displays, and create patches of colour and texture in unexpected places. With a little encouragement, they will dress up the lower branches or base of shrubs whose display is concentrated at a higher level, clothe the forlorn skeleton of a dead tree or drape with greenery a structure that is ugly but immovable.

Those plants that literally climb most surfaces are very few – I can think of only three. Ivy is the most obvious; it comes in a huge and fascinating variety of forms. Its aerial roots will cling to almost anything, but it is best used to cover areas that are ugly but in good condition – it's the best friend a breeze-block wall can have.

Hydrangea petiolaris climbs in a similar way, by means of aerial roots, though initially it needs some help to attach itself to its support. Unlike ivy it is deciduous, though it has the advantage of more showy flowers than ivy can offer.

The third true climber is often called Virginia creeper, which can be confusing as this name is used for two different species; so it is best to stick to botanical names here. The *Parthenocissus* genus of deciduous ornamental vine-like plants has various species that climb and support themselves by means of tendrils. The tendrils do not cling only by twining, as with true vines, but by means of tenaciously adhesive sucker pads (with one exception). P. *quinquefolia* and P. *tricuspidata* are both successful species available in various forms and varieties.

Other so-called trailing and climbing plants need the specific provision of a means of support, such as a trellis, wires or netting, and most of them need to be tied to the support. One criterion, when choosing a plant to climb over a support, should be the amount of trouble you are willing to take. Some plants, such as the honeysuckles, need minimal attention as long as you give them a strong framework to start with and restrain the long shoots once they get going. By contrast, many types of clematis demand much more care and attention from the gardener if they are to look their best.

Ground cover
Other garden nomads travel in a horizontal direction. These include species often referred to as ground cover, such as the mat-forming campanulas. (In fact, many so-called

The rectilinear lines of the trellis contrast strikingly with the luxuriant foliage and the curve of the brilliant pink clematis 'Marcel Moser'.

climbers, such as clematis and ivy, will happily become ground cover if there is nothing for them to climb.) Some of them are more invasive than others. Those, such as *Campanula poscharskyana*, that spread by stolons (above ground), rather than rhizomes (usually below ground) are more easily controlled.

Saponaria ocymoides (tumbling Ted) is another adventurer. Its pretty pink flowers are happy trickling down a wall, but they look even prettier when seen peeping out from among the bluish leaves of a bush of rue.

The periwinkle, usually described as a trailing plant, is another plant whose unpredictable behaviour can make it a joy to have in the garden. When the trails find a likely spot, they root and make new plants. This exploring habit leads the periwinkle in every direction. In my garden it is to be found sprawling among the branches of a prostrate rosemary,

meandering among the primroses and wandering through the lower branches of a variegated holly. I prefer *Vinca minor* to V. *major* because it is a neater plant and because its flowers have a more pronounced propeller-like shape to them.

The usual lilac-blue periwinkle is lovely, but there are also several uncommon forms. I have some with variegated leaves and some with white flowers, and an exotic double-flowered plum-purple one which flowers prolifically.

Like many of the plants I admire, the periwinkle has a respectable history as a medicinal plant. Its botanical name refers to the ancient use of the tough, flexible stems for making wreaths (the Latin verb *vincere* means 'to bind'), so I thought it would be an appropriate plant with which to garland the collar of a blouse.

Clematis

Clematis is similarly suitable for the blind design because it can often be seen trained near windows, and it would not be unusual to see a shoot making its way across a windowsill. The clematis in the design is *Clematis jackmanii*, a very well known hybrid offering plenty of cultivars. I chose it for quite prosaic reasons: the four large 'petals' (which are really sepals) make a simple but dramatic shape which, to an embroiderer, immediately suggests appliqué.

For embroidery design I normally use plants I grow myself, but because of limited space I grow only the wild types of clematis, rather than hybrids, because of the extra value they give. I use C. *armandii* on a warm wall with other climbers to create a jungly effect. In winter, when honeysuckle and jasmine are bare of leaves, this evergreen clematis prevents the wall from looking too forlorn. Its white flowers, though not as showy as those of the larger-flowered types, are

The lesser periwinkle has distinctive blue flowers and glossy green leaves. It spreads profusely and may need cutting back in spring. The sharp outline of the petals and its spreading habit make it an ideal subject for an embroidery motif on the border of a towel, the edges of pillowcases or, as shown on page 60, a blouse collar.

Probably the best known and commonest climbing plant is ivy. Here, a thin covering of frost accentuates the shape of the leaves and the lines of the ribs. With all needlework designs, it is important to study the form of the plant in detail preferably a living specimen.

charming against the glossy leaves, and fragrant as well. C. *armandii* flowers in spring; at the other end of the year, between August and October, come the flowers of my other favourite, C. *flammula*. If you like the scent of vanilla, these flowers are irresistible. When I first smelt them, their strangely antique fragrance had the deeply familiar quality of something recalled from centuries ago. Probably the memory, like so many other perfumed evocations, goes back to childhood, when the sense of smell is so keen.

Embroidery design

Being unfamiliar with C. *jackmanii*, I had to rely on reference books when drawing my design, and I found it more difficult than when referring to a plant I grow myself. Books are useful, but first-hand knowledge is best. Both of the designs used in this chapter, although superficially similar, illustrate the importance of choosing the right plant for your purpose. This applies just as much in embroidery as in the garden. A periwinkle trailing across a blind would probably look insignificant, and most clematis hybrids are too big and bold for use on clothing.

One interesting aspect of this sort of naturalistic design is that it can be reinforced by the use of symmetry. Both the periwinkle and the clematis shoots are drawn very much in the way they grow, without trying to make them conform to a definite pattern. Such designs can be given the decorative force of a pattern by matching them symmetrically, as with the periwinkle. Similarly, the clematis blind would work well as one of a matching pair. The design would look very handsome at the windows of a symmetrically-fronted house with clematis trained around its matching windows. The flowers on the blind could easily be changed to resemble those growing outside.

It is also worthwhile remembering that the means of support provided for climbing and trailing plants can in themselves be useful in embroidery. The regular patterns and formal shapes of trellises, arches, pergolas and other structures can easily be conveyed in stitches as a framework for contrasting, random displays of the plants growing over and through them.

CLEMATIS BLIND

A graceful branch of Clematis jackmanii *winds across this roller blind. Appliqué is well suited to such large-scale, simple shapes; here, the motifs have been applied using transfer fusing web and then embellished with embroidery stitches.*

MAKING THE BLIND

1 Begin by enlarging the diagram overleaf to get the full-size pattern for the stem. The design is shown one-quarter of its actual size. You can either take it to a photocopying service or square it up yourself using the method described on page 139. A simpler approach would be to copy it freehand onto the large piece of paper, using the small version as a guide. If you choose this method, do not transfer the stem design onto the blind until you have cut out the appliqué motifs. Position these on the pattern and adjust the lines of the stem if necessary. Lightly mark the positions of the flowers, buds and leaves on the full-size stem pattern; this will serve as a guide when working the appliqué.

2 Go over the lines of the stem with a heavy black pen. Tape the design to a flat surface, then position the blind fabric over it, with the lower edge about 7cm (2¾ inches) from the bottom. Weight or tape the fabric in place. Using a well-sharpened medium-soft pencil, draw the stem design on the blind fabric.

3 Now trace the patterns for the motifs onto the transfer fusing web (or ordinary web): 3 flowers, 2 buds and 16 leaves. The leaves are of slightly different sizes and shapes; four basic patterns are given, the smaller ones being intended for the stems with buds.

It is suggested that you use 2 of each larger leaf, 4 medium and 8 small, but you can, of course, vary this to suit yourself. You may also wish to adapt the tracings slightly in order to achieve the natural quality of the original. When tracing, place the transfer fusing web paper-side down, and position the motifs close together. Use a ballpoint or fine fibre-tip pen, and make sure that the line is visible on the paper. Do *not* cut out the motifs. (However, if you are using ordinary web, do cut them out.)

4 Cut roughly around each group of motifs. Place each piece on the wrong side of the appropriate fabric and iron them onto it, following the manufacturer's instructions. Cut out the shapes. (If using ordinary fusing web, make paper tracings of the motifs, and use the tracings as patterns to cut the motifs in fabric. Pin each motif to its corresponding web shape.)

5 Mount the fabric on the frame (see Note).

MATERIALS

Roller blind (window shade) kit for a blind about 90cm (3 feet) wide; one with ready-stiffened fabric is easier to work on, but it is possible to work on unstiffened fabric and apply a stiffening solution afterwards.

Fabrics for appliqué: 20cm (¼ yard) of mauve and 10cm (⅛ yard) of green; the most suitable is a lightweight to medium-weight, closely woven natural-fibre fabric that does not fray easily. Remember that the colour will appear darker when silhouetted against the sun.

2.5m (2¾ yards) of flat, narrow brown braid or knitting yarn

Stranded cotton (floss) to match appliqué fabrics and braid, plus lime green (1 skein each)

Medium-sized crewel needle

Transfer or ordinary fusing web

Piece of paper at least 86 by 36cm (34 by 14 inches)

Black ballpoint or fine fibre-tip pen

Heavy black fibre-tip pen

Medium-soft pencil

Rectangular frame (see Note)

Size of embroidery design: approximately 86cm (34 inches) in length.

The trace diagram is one-quarter actual size and has been divided into two. The blue lines indicate where the two parts of the diagram overlap. Enlarge and trace each part separately and then match the overlapping sections.

6 Apply the braid to the stem design, using a fine running stitch and 2 strands of floss. Be generous with the braid; don't cut off the end before you reach the position of the leaf or flower, and leave 5mm (¼ inch), which will go under the edge of the motif. If you are using yarn, couch it in place, using the stranded floss and placing the stitches about 1–1.5cm (⅜ to ⅝ inch) apart.

7 Position the motifs on the blind, using the full-size design as a guide. Peel away the paper backing and iron each motif in place. (The work is left on the frame during this process; either a table or an ironing board can be used for the pressing.)

8 Using 2 strands of floss and the matching colours, work around all the shapes in slanting satin stitch

(or, if you prefer, buttonhole stitch). Finish the ends neatly on the wrong side; not only will the window side of the blind be visible from outside, but light shining through it will reveal any messy bits.

9 Mark a circle with a diameter of about 1.5cm (⅝ inch) in the centre of each flower. Using 2 strands of lime green floss, fill the circles with French knots. Start with a ring at the edge, and work in towards the centre. Wrap the thread twice round the needle.

10 Remove the blind from the frame. If necessary, sponge it carefully with a weak solution of liquid detergent to freshen it and remove any distortion; then sponge with clear water. Allow the work to dry, and press it carefully at a medium-hot setting,

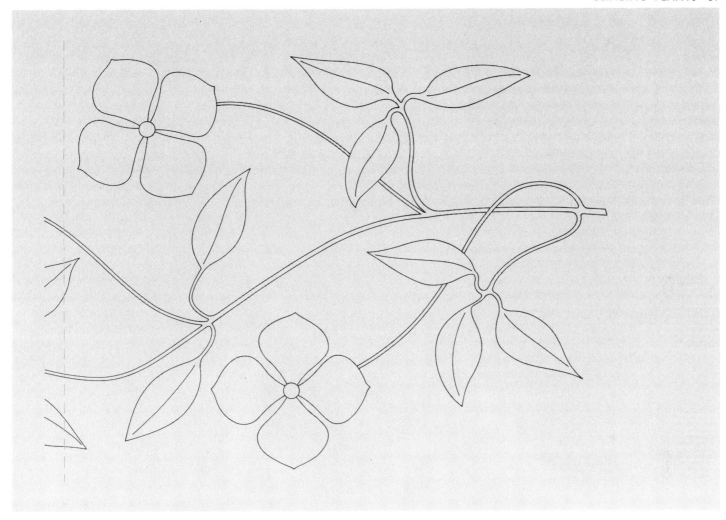

preferably using a steam iron.

11 Assemble the blind according to the manufacturer's instructions.

Note If you are working on pre-stiffened fabric, you will not need to tension the fabric in the usual way. However, it will need to be supported, and the excess fabric should be rolled up out of the way. If you own (or have access to) a large, rectangular quilting frame, the fabric can be mounted on this. Alternatively, if you have a scroll frame, you can substitute some home-made extra-long rollers, cut from dowelling. The dowelling should be at least 1.5cm ($\frac{1}{2}$ inch) longer than the width of the blind and at least 2cm ($\frac{3}{4}$ inch) in diameter. If the frame is the

type in which the rollers slot through the sides, the dowelling can be treated in the same way; if not, tie the dowelling to the sides with strong twine.

To attach the fabric, first staple or tape the upper edge of the fabric to the top roller, then roll the fabric up carefully and tightly until the lower edge rests on the lower roller. Using an ordinary sewing needle and fine, strong thread, sew it over the roller; make the stitching neat, to avoid distorting the fabric; this edge will show. Because the fabric is stiff, there is no need to attach it to the sides of the frame, but tension the rollers slightly.

If you are using unstiffened fabric, you should cut it slightly wider than required, so that it can be attached to the sides and tensioned in the usual way.

PERIWINKLE BLOUSE

A spray of periwinkle makes an attractive design for embroidery on a shawl-collared blouse like the one shown here. The design could be shortened or modified in some other way to suit a different shape of collar.

MATERIALS

Blouse pattern with shawl collar
Fabric, buttons, thread, as required; the fabric
  should be fairly lightweight and closely woven;
  cotton or linen is most successful.
DMC stranded cotton (floss) in the following
  colours: 987, 471, 632, 340, 343 and 741 (one
  skein each)
Fine crewel needle
Good-quality tracing paper
Pen
Medium (HB) pencil
Scroll or rectangular frame.

WORKING THE EMBROIDERY

1 Make a tracing of the collar piece of the pattern. Mark the seam allowance and foldline, if any, so that the finished visible area of the collar is clearly indicated.

2 Enlarge the diagram (far right) to its actual size. Place the tracing over the design, with the left side (i.e. the side on the wearer's left) facing upwards, positioning the design in the most attractive manner, within the finished area. Trace the design using a pen. If it needs to be modified, lightly mark the modifications in pencil; when satisfied with them, go over the lines with a pen.

3 Tape the tracing to a window with sunlight behind it. Cut a piece of fabric (prepared as appropriate – see page 139) large enough to accommodate both left and right collar pieces and to fit the frame. Tape this over the tracing and trace the motif and the outer edge of the collar pattern. For the right collar section, reverse the tracing on the window, then trace the design onto the fabric as before. (For authenticity, you may wish to use the unreversed left-side flower and bud, because these always turn in an anti-clockwise direction.)

4 Mount the fabric on the frame.

5 Work the embroidery using 1 strand of floss throughout (2 strands can be used if preferred; this will make the work faster but slightly less smooth.) It is best to work both sides together, a little at a time, this helps to ensure a close match when angling the stitches. Begin by working the main stems in 632 and then the smaller ones in 471, using slanting satin stitch throughout.

6 Work the sepals enclosing the flower buds in 471 in detached chain stitches, with an extra straight stitch at the side, sloped to form a 'V'.

7 Work the leaves in satin stitch, using 987, slanting the stitches outwards and downwards from the central vein at the top towards the lower tip of the leaf.

8 Work the flowers in split stitch, following the shape of the petals (see detail photograph) and using 340. Finish the flowers by working 4 straight stitches, crossing these over each other at the centre.

9 Work the flower buds also in split stitch: first work the lines marking the folded petals, using 343; then fill in with 340.

10 When the embroidery is complete, remove the work from the frame; wash it and press it carefully over a thick soft pad to flatten any puckers around the embroidery.

11 Make up the blouse as instructed by the pattern.

▲ The flowers and buds are worked in split stitch using one or two strands of violet-blue floss.

▶ The trace diagram is shown half actual size. Enlarge and trace it off before making any adjustments to the design.

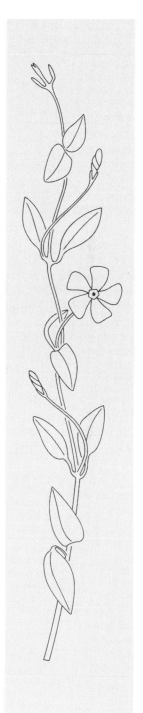

$\mathcal{T}$HE SCENTED GARDEN

Most of us can trace at least some of our adult tastes and preferences back to childhood. From a very early age I was fascinated by smells of all sorts. I had an unusually good sense of smell and I was often rebuked for using my nose to identify unknown substances – a habit best kept for recognizing different flowers.

One of my earliest memories is of the nasturtiums my father planted to grow up over the air raid shelter at the bottom of our garden (a relic of the war). It's not their colours I remember, but the lovely spicy, not-too-sweet smell. When, later, I sowed children's traditional seed mixture of cornflowers and pot marigolds, they grew and I picked the flowers. The calendulas had a resinous stickiness about their stems and leaves which captivated me. It clung to my hands, and I used to bury my nose in my cupped palms to inhale the strangely satisfying perfume.

Today one of my interests is to look out for the bits and pieces that come out of old work boxes; the general paraphernalia of sewing is something I will always find absorbing. My grandmother taught me to knit and sew when I was quite young and I used to seize the chance to poke about in her mahogany workbox and see what I could find. On one occasion I discovered an old and fragile lavender sachet, its contents spilling out. When I had scraped up some of the faded, dusty grains, I rolled them between my finger and thumb and sniffed them; even after all those years inside the box they were still surpris-

ingly pungent. I think that was when the scent of lavender—one of my favourites—first became lodged in my brain.

Plants for pillows and sachets

Most of us would not be without such plants as honeysuckle and jasmine for their unpredictable wafts of sweetness. Lots of lovely scents are best after dark and we need warm evenings to savour them. Many plants with aromatic leaves are less than generous with their fragrance, but I enjoy a 'pinch and crush' tour of a garden, to seek out those scents that keep themselves to themselves. Bay leaves in particular have a wonderful aroma, useful in cooking, but best appreciated after a good sniff when the freshly-crushed leaf is still warm from the sun.

For many gardeners a plant's fragrance is not simply a bonus but the main reason for its inclusion. My own garden would be half empty if I were to remove all the plants chosen primarily for their perfumed flowers or aromatic foliage.

The scented plants that are of special interest to the embroiderer are the relatively few that retain their fragrance after drying, such as lavender and roses. (The scent of lavender is perhaps best appreciated in its dried form.) The dried flowers and leaves of such plants can be used to fill sachets and pillows, giving a pleasant fragrance to a bed-

This brilliant display of delphiniums and sweet peas is not only eye-catching, but the flowers yield a sweet scent on warm evenings.

Honeysuckle is one of the loveliest plants in the scented garden. Keep the roots shaded but, if possible, choose a position where the top growth can reach full sun. The woodbine or common honeysuckle (*Lonicera periclymenum*) shown here is a twining kind that lends itself to embroidery designs on bed linen, tablecloths and even blinds and curtains. A single flower motif would look pretty on table napkins or a handkerchief.

room, linen drawer or cupboard all the year round. Such objects make welcome presents, and they are a special pleasure to make; for the scent, colours and forms of the plant can all be delightfully combined into a single harmonious piece of work.

The aromatic essential oils released by scented plants smell subtly different to every nose, and they vary from plant to plant of the same name, and throughout the year. Inevitably, of course, one's climate imposes limitations. For example, the delicious scent of citrus trees in bloom can only be a fantasy or a memory for those of us who live in colder northern latitudes – unless we are lucky enough to have a large conservatory. People who live around the Mediterranean or in Florida or California, on the other hand, may take the sharp sweet smell of oranges and lemons for granted, in the same way that English people think of Bramley apples, for example. I still remember the thrill of picking a lemon from a tree in February, while I was

working in Portugal, and breathing in the heady scent of the blossoms.

The next best thing to having one's own lemon grove is to grow some of the various lemon-scented plants that will thrive in a cool climate. Among these are lemon verbena, lemon balm and lemon geranium, all of which have been used in the cushion shown on page 67. There is also a member of the catmint family, *Nepeta giovaniana*, which has lovely lemon-scented leaves and pretty yellow flowers. My own favourite among these is lemon verbena (*Aloysia triphylla*); the fragrance of its crushed leaves is as delicious as lemon meringue pie (but not as fattening). However, this plant can be difficult to please, so if you favour an easy life, you might go for lemon balm instead.

Another pungent plant that lends itself well to drying is the orange or eau-de-cologne mint. This keeps its strong fragrance for a long time and is ideal for scenting drawers and wardrobes.

◄ The fragrant silvery-grey foliage of artemisia would make an appropriate and pleasing needlework design on a sachet for a linen chest or drawer. The leaves can be dried and used to fill the sachet. The plant shown here, growing between the smooth, irregularly shaped stones of a path, might inspire an embroidered design on patchwork.

Of the various plants used for potpourri, lavender and old roses are the most popular; and their beauty makes them welcome additions to the garden irrespective of their scent. Other good ingredients for potpourri are the commoner catmints, *Nepeta faassenii* and *Nepeta mussinii*.

Also well worth including in the scented garden are *Caryopteris × clandonensis* (Blue Spiraea) and *Perovskia atriplicifolia* (Russian sage), shrubs which can be treated as herbaceous perennials and cut hard back in early spring in the same way as buddleia. They both have unusual foliage which is deliciously aromatic. Most of the artemisias also have leaves that can be used in scented sachets for lingerie drawers and linen chests.

A somewhat under-used plant, woodruff has several virtues for the gardener and embroiderer alike. It provides excellent ground cover for spring bulbs when they are dying down, and its pretty star-shaped flowers and leaves make attractive embroidery motifs. Most references to woodruff in books state that it releases its aroma of new-mown hay only as it dies down; but I have a bank of woodruff that smells heavenly when in full fresh leaf. The dried plant tops are also springy enough to make a good stuffing, and I have used these – along with a few other herbs – to fill the little boudoir pillow shown on page 75.

When using dried plants as fillings for sachets and pillows, make sure to dry them thoroughly; otherwise unpleasant-smelling and unattractive moulds may grow. Aromatic leaves should be picked just before the plant flowers for the most concentrated scent. Pick them in the morning after the dew has dried but before the sun is at its highest. Either hang them up or spread them out to dry completely.

Roses are undoubtedly many people's favourite flowers both because of the beauty of their blooms and their delicious, heady fragrance. They are among the few flowers that retain their scent when the petals are dried and are, therefore, often used in making potpourri. Roses have long been an inspiration to embroiderers, and fine examples of fifteenth- and sixteenth-century needlework featuring both realistic and stylized rose designs may be seen in museums and stately homes. They were also popular in mass-produced embroidery designs in the nineteenth century. A single flower or a group of blooms would make a delightful picture, cushion cover or greeting card. Roses also make pretty border designs on table linen and bed linen.

CITRUS CUSHION

Zingy citrus colours – orange, lemon yellow and lime green – are used for the embroidery on this cushion, which features the leaves of the lemon geranium. The dried leaves of this plant, along with those of two other plants, lemon verbena and lemon balm, give the cushion its fragrance.

WORKING THE EMBROIDERY

(**Note:** When referring to fabric, the words 'thread' and 'threads' here refer to pairs of threads.)
1 Cut a piece of the fabric measuring 48cm (19 inches) square. Neaten the edges and mark the vertical and horizontal centres with lines of tacking (basting).
2 Mount the fabric in the frame, not too tightly.
3 **(outer yellow square)** Count out 122 threads from the centre on each arm of the cross, and tack (baste) a square joining these points. This marks the inner edge of the outer yellow square.
4 Using a long strand of the yellow no.5 perlé cotton, work double chain stitch (see diagram A) just outside the tacked line. Work the stitching over

MATERIALS

50cm (⅝ yard) of hardanger fabric, with 22 paired threads to 2.5cm (1 inch)
3 skeins of no.5 perlé cotton in lemon yellow; the shade used here is DMC 444
1 skein each of no.5 perlé cotton in bright orange and lime green; shades used are DMC 608 and 907
1 skein each of no.3 perlé cotton in lemon yellow and bright orange
1 skein of no.8 perlé cotton in lemon yellow
1 skein of stranded cotton (floss) in lemon yellow

Medium-sized tapestry needle
40cm (½ yard) of muslin or other thin cotton fabric
Cushion pad (pillow form) 40cm (16 inches) square
About 280g (3 oz) of dried leaves of lemon-scented plants
38cm (15 inch) zip fastener
Thin tracing or tissue paper
Water-erasable pen
Ruler
Slate or rectangular frame

Size of finished cushion: approximately 42cm (16½ inches) square.

6 fabric threads, and 'overlap' the lines at the corners as shown in the detail photograph.

5 (outer orange diamond) Starting at the outer edge of the yellow square, count along one of the tacked lines 58 fabric threads. Mark this point with a pin. Now count diagonally upwards to the right over groups of 4 thread intersections until you are 6 threads from the yellow square; mark this point also with a pin. Using orange no.5 perlé cotton, work backstitch over 4 threads, working from the yellow square down to the first point (2 threads at the top are unworked). Continue up diagonally to the left in the same way.

6 Work another line of backstitch 4 fabric threads up from the first line.

7 Using no.3 orange perlé cotton, work loops through the backstitch as shown in Diagram B. Repeat steps 5–7 on each side of the square.

8 (middle orange diamond) Count up 3 fabric threads from the yellow square on each arm of the cross; mark these points with pins. Join them with diagonal lines of backstitch over 4 threads, using no.5 orange perlé. Work another line inside this line, as in step 6. then thread these stitches with no.3 as shown in Diagram C.

9 (inner orange diamond) Count 56 fabric threads out from the centre of the cross in each direction. Work the outer line of backstitch as before, then the inner line (slightly different from previously) as shown in Diagram D. Thread these stitches with no.3 perlé as shown in the diagram.

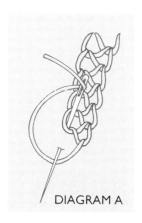

◀ **Double chain stitch** is worked downwards alternately from left to right. Here it is worked over 6 threads across and 4 threads downwards.

DIAGRAM A

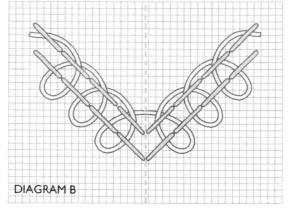

DIAGRAM B

▲ Detail showing the position of one leaf motif. The outline is worked in small stem stitches and one stitch is worked over another in a 'y' shape at the corners. The stitching is then whipped with one strand of floss to make a graphic outline.

◀ **Diagram B** – outer orange diamond: work loops through 2 lines of backstitch 4 fabric threads apart, as shown.

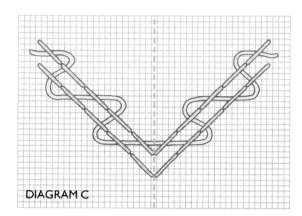

DIAGRAM C

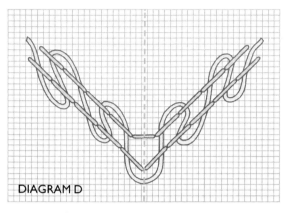

DIAGRAM D

◄◄ Diagram C – middle orange diamond: work loops through 2 lines of backstitch 4 fabric threads apart as shown.

◄ Diagram D – inner orange diamond: work 2 lines of backstitch with the stitches opposite, not staggered. Work loops as shown.

▼ Trace the leaf motif (actual size) four times. with a water erasable pen and a ruler, mark diagonals through each corner section and tack (baste) one tracing in position, aligning the stalk with the diagonal.

10 **(middle yellow square)** Count outwards 74 threads from the centre of the cross in each direction. Work lines of tacking (basting) outwards from these points. This marks the inner edge of the square. Using yellow no.5 perlé, work 2 lines of blanket stitch over 6 threads, as shown in Diagram E; then thread the stitches with no.3 perlé.

11 **(inner yellow square)** Using no.5 yellow perlé, work 2 interlocking rows of blanket stitch as shown in Diagram F. Note that the stitches are worked into the same holes on each row. Using no.3 perlé, work backstitch down the centre of the stitches as shown in the diagram, thus separating the vertical strands of the blanket stitches.

12 **(leaf motifs)** Trace the leaf design 4 times. Using the ruler and water-erasable pen, mark diagonals through each corner section. Tack (baste) each tracing to a corner section, aligning the stalk with the diagonal.

13 Using a long strand of the yellow no.8 perlé, work the outline of each leaf in small stem stitches. Keep the stitching fairly tight on the straight sections, but looser on the tight curves, adding an extra stitch or two where necessary. At the inner corners, work one stitch over another in a 'y' shape (see detail photograph opposite). Whip the stitching with one strand of the yellow floss, using tiny stitches. This will pull the outline into shape, giving a neat and graphic line which contrasts well with the geometric border.

14 **(darning)** Finally, darn the background, using the no.5 green perlé cotton and working over 5 threads

and under 1. Change the direction of the darning on the diagonal lines at the corners.

MAKING UP THE CUSHION
1 Wash the embroidery in the frame (see page 141), and leave it to dry.
2 Remove the work from the frame, and trim the

The background between the inner yellow square and inner orange diamond is darned in green perlé cotton.

edges, leaving a piece 46cm (18 inches) square. Cut another piece of fabric the same size. Work zigzag stitch or oversewing over all edges.

3 Make up the cushion cover as described on page 141, inserting a zip fastener.

4 Make a twisted cord from the two remaining skeins of yellow no.5 perlé cotton (see page 142), and sew it to the front of the cover.

5 Cut the muslin to measure 40 by 80cm (16 by 32 inches). Fold this in half widthwise, and stitch around the edges, leaving a small gap. Turn this bag right side out, and fill it with the mixture of dried herbs. Stitch up the gap.

6 Insert the cushion pad (pillow form) into the cover, then slip the bag of herbs between the pad and the embroidery, smoothing out the leaves so that they lie flat. When the zip is closed, the leaves will stay in place.

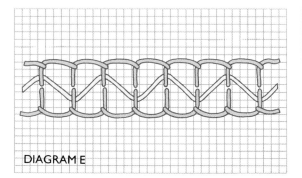

DIAGRAM E

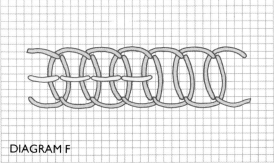

DIAGRAM F

◀◀ **Diagram E** – middle yellow square: work 2 lines of blanket stitch over 6 fabric threads. Thread as shown.

◀ **Diagram F** – inner yellow square: work 2 interlocking rows of blanket stitch. Work backstitch along the centre.

LAVENDER SACHET

The scent of lavender is one of the most evocative ways to perfume linen or keep moths away from clothes. The pungent dried flower buds of Lavandula angustifolia *'Nana Alba', used for this sachet, won't need replacing for at least a year.*

PREPARATION

I Prepare the fabric as appropriate (see page 139).
2 Trace the design given overleaf, then transfer the tracing twice onto the fabric, using the dressmaker's carbon and positioning each oval so that it can be framed with a good margin all round.
3 Thread up the sewing machine with any colour of thread, and stitch around all three ovals on both sections, using a stitch length of about 2mm (scant $\frac{1}{8}$ inch). Tighten the upper tension very slightly; this will make it easier to remove the stitches. Do not secure the ends, and leave short lengths on the outer line, which will be used for gathering. (If you do not have a machine, work this outer line in small running stitches; the other lines can be marked with a water-erasable pen.)
4 Mount the fabric in the frame.

MATERIALS

Piece of plain-woven lavender-coloured cotton
   or linen about 45 by 30cm (18 by 12 inches)
Stranded cotton (floss) in white, pink, green and
   two shades of blue; the shades used here are
   DMC white, 605, 502, 340 and 333, respectively
Coton à broder in white
10cm (4 inches) of narrow lavender-coloured
   ribbon
Medium-sized crewel needle
Fine tapestry needle
Ring frame
Tracing paper
Dressmaker's carbon paper
Piece of writing paper
Dried lavender sachet

Size of finished sachet: approximately 11 by 8cm
   ($4\frac{1}{2}$ by 3 inches)

WORKING THE EMBROIDERY

Work each motif in turn.

I Work the lavender buds in seeding, using 2 strands of floss in the crewel needle and working 2 stitches into the holes. Scatter the colours – white, pink, and two shades of blue – randomly, using the photograph as a guide. Avoid pulling the stitches tightly.
2 Using 2 strands of green floss in the needle, work running stitch around the inner oval, pulling out the machine stitching about 3cm (1 inch) at a time as you go round.
3 Using the tapestry needle, thread 4 strands of the green floss through the running stitches.
4 Repeat steps 1–3 on the other motif.

MAKING UP THE SACHET

I Remove the work from the frame, and cut out the motifs, about 3–4mm (scant $\frac{1}{4}$ inch) from the outer line of stitching.
2 Trace the middle-sized oval from the design, and use the tracing to draw two oval templates on the writing paper. Cut these out.
3 Draw up the gathering threads slightly on the motif, turning the edge to the wrong side, and insert the template. Continue drawing up the threads, adjusting the gathers evenly, until the gathered edge fits smoothly over the template; the middle line of stitching should lie on the edge. Tie the ends of the gathering thread, and remove the middle line of stitching. Press the work from the wrong side; remove the template carefully and press again. Repeat step 3 with the other motif. (This process may seem somewhat fiddly, but it is important because turning under the edge of an oval neatly and evenly so that it lies flat is very difficult without the help of a template.)

4 Machine stitch around the turned-under edge of each section, using a stitch length of about 3mm ($\frac{1}{8}$ inch) and working the same distance from the edge. (This stitching, too, will serve only as a guide so the colour is immaterial.)

5 Pulling out the machine stitching as you go, work blanket stitch around the edge of each oval, using a single strand of coton à broder and working into the holes left by the machine stitching. Work backstitch to join the 'legs' of the blanket stitch, creating a ladder effect. On the wrong side, trim the fabric close to the stitching.

6 Sew the piece of ribbon to the top of one oval, forming a loop.

7 Place the two ovals together, with wrong sides facing, and oversew them together, using coton à broder and working through the edges of the blanket stitch. When only a small gap remains, fill this with the lavender, then complete the stitching. Press the edges with your fingers, to mould the sachet into shape.

Note: A traditional mixture for moth sachets includes, besides lavender, a pinch each of dried thyme and mint, ground cloves, caraway and salt.

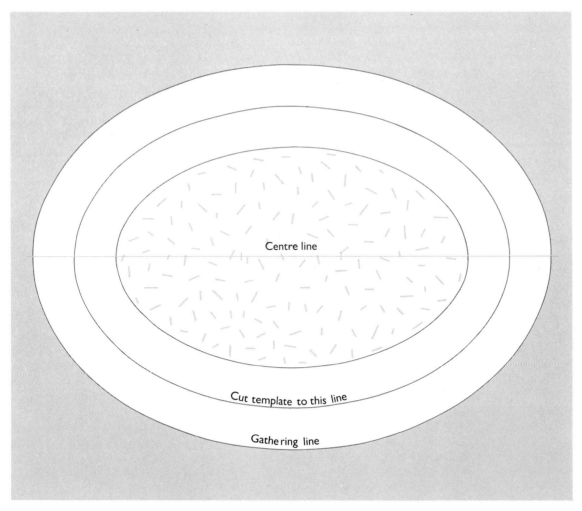

Trace the design (actual size) and transfer it twice onto the fabric using dressmaker's carbon, making sure to mark all three ovals. Trace the middle-sized oval (the line marked 'cut template to this line') and use to draw two templates on writing paper.

Centre line

Cut template to this line

Gathering line

WOODRUFF PILLOW

The delicate star-like flowers, gracefully tapering leaves and straight stems of the woodruff plant form the design of this little pillow, which is filled with a mixture of woodruff and other herbs.

PREPARING THE FABRIC

1 Prepare the fabric as described on page 139. Cut a piece 45cm (18 inches) square, or large enough to fit the frame, and reinforce the edges.

2 Trace the diagram on page 76 4 times, using the transfer pencil and pivoting the tracing paper around the centre point (do not reverse it) to make the complete pattern for the embroidery.

3 Place the tracing face down on the fabric, aligning the notches with the lengthwise and crosswise grains, and tack (baste) it in place through the centre in both directions and around the edges. Iron the design onto the fabric, taking care not to slide the iron over the surface. Undo a few tacking stitches at the edge, and check to make sure the design has transferred before removing all the tacking. Keep

MATERIALS

50cm (½ yard) of white linen sheeting or other plain-woven linen or cotton fabric, at least 138cm (54 inches) wide

1 skein of white stranded cotton (floss)

1 skein of white no.5 perlé cotton

1 skein of white no.12 perlé cotton (if obtainable; otherwise use 2 strands of floss)

1 skein of white coton à broder

30cm (⅜ yard) of calico (unbleached muslin)

Fine and medium-sized crewel needles

Tracing paper

Embroidery transfer pencil

Embroidery frame (any type) with an area large enough to accommodate whole design

Approximately 200g (8 ounces) of dried herbal sachet; the mixture used for this pillow is mainly woodruff with a little lavender and wormwood; some cotton wool (absorbent cotton) was added for softness

6 small press studs (snaps)

Size of finished pillow: approximately 28cm (11 inches) in diameter, excluding frill.

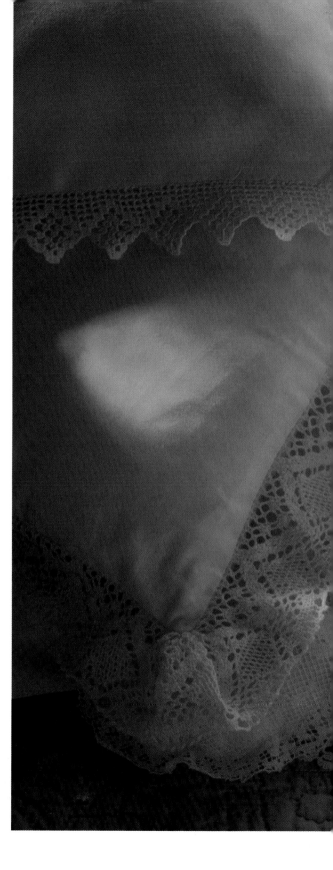

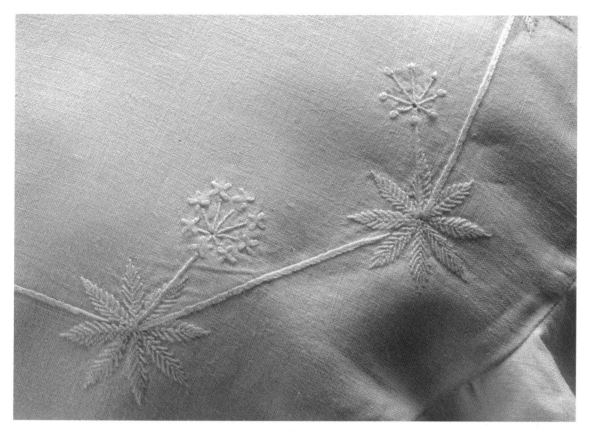

◀◀ Trace the design four times, pivoting the tracing paper to make the complete pattern. Do not reverse the design. Place the tracing face down onto the fabric and iron on the design.

◀ The flower and seed head stems are worked in whipped stem stitch; the seeds in French knots; the flower heads in straight stitches; the leaves in fly stitch; and the long stems are couched.

this pattern for use later.
4 Mount the fabric in the frame.

WORKING THE EMBROIDERY
1 Begin by working the seed heads. For the stems use one strand of the floss and work in stem stitch, then whip the stitching in the same thread, pulling the stitches fairly tightly. The seeds are French knots worked in coton à broder, with the thread taken twice around the needle.
2 Work the flower heads. Using no.5 perlé cotton, work 4 short straight stitches for each individual flower. Work the stems as for the seed heads.
3 Work the leaves in no.12 perlé cotton (or 2 strands of floss). Start at the top with one straight stitch, then work fly stitch to the base, placing the stitches close together and making the tying stitches about 1–2mm ($\frac{1}{16}$ inch) long.

4 Work the flower stems in whipped stem stitch, using coton à broder and pulling the whipping stitches tightly.
5 The long stems are worked in couching. Lay 2 strands of coton à broder, and couch them with fly stitches, using a single strand of floss and placing the stitches about 3–4mm (generous $\frac{1}{8}$ inch) apart.
6 Remove the embroidery from the frame. Wash it carefully, if necessary, and press it, equally carefully, from the wrong side over a thick pad. Trim around the marked edge.

MAKING UP THE PILLOW
1 Using your pattern, cut another circle of linen for the back of the pillow cover and 2 circles of calico (unbleached muslin) for the pillow pad.
2 Trace the pattern for the frill, and cut it 4 times in the linen, placing the straight line at a 45° angle to

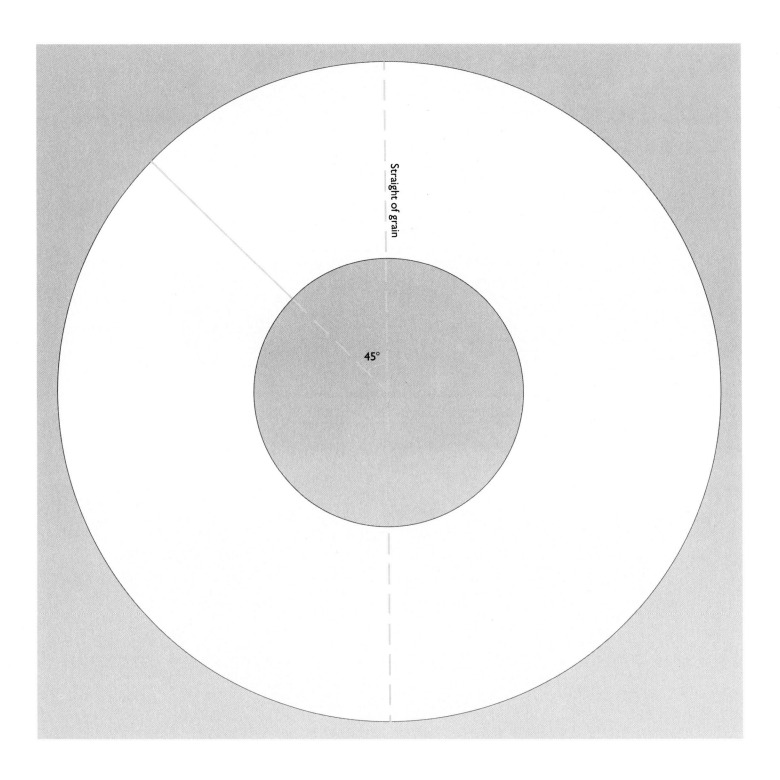

Straight of grain

45°

the grain. Cut out the frill pieces.

3 Join the four sections of the frill end to end, taking 3mm ($\frac{1}{8}$ inch) seam allowance. Press the seams open.

4 Turn under and press a 1 cm ($\frac{3}{8}$ inch) hem around the edge of the frill; stitch it in place by machine, using either ordinary topstitch or a decorative edging such as shell stitch.

5 Place the frill over the embroidered cover with right sides facing, raw edges matching and the seams aligned with notches. Pin them together at these four points, then continue pinning in between these points, easing the fullness on the frill to fit the edge of the cover. Tack (baste) the frill in place.

6 On the back cover piece, mark off one-quarter of the circumference. Clip to a depth of nearly 1 cm ($\frac{3}{8}$ inch) at each end, then turn under and tack (baste)

a 1cm ($\frac{3}{8}$ inch) hem. Topstitch the hem in place.

7 Place the front and back sections together with right sides facing and with the frill sandwiched in between them. Pin, tack (baste) and machine stitch, taking 1cm ($\frac{3}{8}$ inch) seam allowance and leaving the hemmed edge of the back cover free. Reinforce the stitching at both ends.

8 Sew the press studs (snaps) to both sides of the cover along the edges.

9 Pin, tack (baste) and stitch the two sections of the pillow pad together, leaving about 8cm (3 inches) open. Turn the pad right side, out, and fill it with the herb mixture. Sew up the gap by hand, with oversewing stitches. When the herbs eventually need replacing, simply undo these stitches.

10 Slip the pad into the embroidered cover.

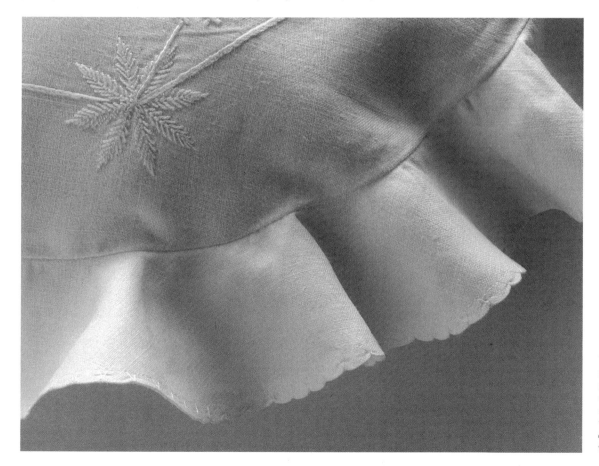

Trace the pattern for the frill (opposite) and cut out 4 frill pieces, placing the straight cutting line 45° to the straight of grain. When joining the frill to the embroidered cover (see detail), carefully ease the fullness to fit.

BUDS AND BLOOMS

I have often wondered why, like most gardeners, I find buds so tantalizing. They evoke the same thrill of pleasure as a gift waiting to be unwrapped – and yet there can be no mystery as to their contents. Even with a plant new to my garden, I know very well what to expect in the way of flowers (or I should not have bought it in the first place). Every gardener is familiar with snowdrops and daffodils, and yet each passing spring only increases the delight of waiting for the flowers to emerge.

A flower in bud is often more exciting than a full bloom, because it invites anticipation of beauty to come, while being lovely in its own right. Buds are concentrated versions of their subsequent forms, often with a dark tint which is diluted by the opening of the petals.

Part of the attraction of flowers for the embroiderer must lie in the variety of colour, size and form which they offer. They vary in the shape, number and texture of their petals, and the diversity of their reproductive apparatus is impressive (reproduction being the reason for the existence of flowers in the first place). This variety means that some types are easier than others to convey in embroidery. Once a plant is in full bloom, its form may be obscured by the mass of petals, sepals and so on, and it is difficult to decide how to depict a plant if its underlying structure is not apparent.

This is where buds can be a useful alternative. Because they are tight and compact, buds are easy to embroider. They can often be suggested very effectively, in small-scale work, by French knots or detached chain stitches. Many plants of the labiate family, which includes a number of herbs and aromatic plants, have long flower spikes made up of lots of tiny lipped flowers which are complicated to embroider. Several larger plants, such as delphiniums, hollyhocks and gladioli, have a similar structure. All these are much less daunting to portray if you look at them when they are in bud, or when just one or two of the flowers have opened.

It is difficult to believe that the elaborate flower of this blooming camellia was once packed inside such a neat bud.

The flower spikes of veronica open from the bottom upwards. It is easier – and less work – to capture the quintessential qualities of the plant in embroidery at this stage.

Elaborate, realistic representations of flowers are often very satisfying to work and lovely to look at, but there is a different satisfaction in finding a simple way of conveying the essential characteristics of a particular flower. Study any flower as it develops from bud to bloom, and you may find that even the most complex inflorescence becomes simple to embroider if you catch it in bud.

Individual flowers open in succession, until each plant's quota of buds has been exhausted. Where the flowers are grouped to form a larger flowerhead, there is a progression of bloom, usually from base to tip. There are exceptions: *Liatris* flowers (common names button snakeroot, Kansas gayfeather or blazing star) open from the top downwards. Teasel and plantain flowers open in rings surrounding the flower head, each ring dying off as a new one shows its colours.

Form, diversity and design

Just as flowers vary, so do buds. Basically, buds consist of sepals, usually green, enclosing tightly folded petals and the working parts of the flower. Some flowers fool us – the large, brightly coloured 'petals' of the clematis are not petals at all, but over-sized sepals. In some other flowers, hibiscus, statice and helichrysum, for example, the bracts or calices are bigger and more colourful than the insignificant flowers. Nevertheless, a bud is a bud, but not all buds have the same way of revealing the flower inside.

Most flowers force the sepals apart while they are still attached to the stem, but eschscholzias and some poppies have sepals which form little hoods that pop off the opening flowers. Some blossoms, particularly apple blossom, seem to arrange the still-closed buds like ornaments around the newly-opened central flower of a cluster. When blossom continues over a long season, as with citrus fruit trees and myrtle bushes,

Trees often feature in larger gardens, but incorporating an entire tree in an embroidery design could be very tricky. One way of using trees in needlework would be to base a design on the flowers. Catkins are often pretty shapes and, when still mainly in bud, can be embroidered very simply.

The small, tight buds of grape hyacinths may be interpreted by a cluster of French knots arranged in a spiral shape up the spike. Shown here is a very popular blue variety, but other kinds may be white, violet, purple and even yellow.

there is a very decorative quality in the display of new buds, open flowers and fruit on the same plant at the same time.

Double-flowered varieties are especially attractive when their buds are just opening. The German term for such flowers is *Gefüllt* (filled) which is a much more apt description – how can so many frilly layers be crammed into such a tiny parcel? Double opium poppies are good examples of this.

We should not forget trees as a source of flowers for embroidery design. Catkins, particularly from alder and hazel trees, are pretty; when in bud, before they go long and floppy and scatter pollen, they immediately suggest the use of Cretan stitch. Several types of pine cone, which are, in effect, flowers, are equally suitable. Several varieties of acacia give us the fluffy yellow balls more often known as mimosa flowers, and these are a gift to an embroiderer.

Reviving tradition

Because they are simple in shape, buds lend themselves to informal designs. Different sorts of buds can be grouped to make a small posy or nosegay design. They are ideal for use as random patterns or to make scattered backgrounds for more elaborate motifs. They can be used as part of a border design for a picture or a sampler depicting a full-opened flower or an entire plant. Studying the details of different buds and the way they open will add authenticity to all your work.

The shape of many flowers can be reduced to a disc, which makes them excellent designs for buttons. The variety and overall quality of purchased buttons are not as good as they used to be; and for a hand-embroidered blouse or a hand-knitted sweater, specially-made buttons provide an unusual finishing touch, where an ordinary plastic button could be a bit disappointing

Brooches made on different sizes of metal

or plastic rings have a rather touching naiveté about them. Such brooches were popular during World War II, when clothes and personal ornaments were scarce. The design is based on a posy or nosegay of buds of different shapes and colours, and a brooch like those shown on page 89 would make a pretty accessory on a spring suit, for example.

Lavendula stoechas has inflorescences like tiny pine cones, studded with minuscule indigo flowers and topped with purple bracts.

BLOSSOM BUTTONS & BUTTONS ON RINGS

By working over plastic button frames in different-coloured threads, using a variety of stitches, you can create all sorts of charming blossom-motif buttons. Simple metal rings, covered with buttonhole stitch, can also be made into French-knot buttons.

MAKING THE BLOSSOM BUTTONS

1 Using the main embroidery thread and the larger needle, work around the ring. (The buttons in the photograph opposite were made using a small, 15mm [$\frac{5}{8}$ inch] frame.) Hold the end of the thread with your thumb until you have worked a few stitches; when you reach the starting point, tie the ends together on the underside of the button.

2 The centre will be empty. To fill it, work a few stitches across it in one direction, using a single strand of the floss, then a few more, at a right-angle to the first, thus forming a network of threads.

3 Then work French knots on this network base, using a heavier thread.

Alternatives Instead of working the centres as described in steps 2 and 3, you can simply work stitches in a contrasting colour over the centre, working back and forth in a clockwise or anti-clockwise direction. A single French knot can then be worked at the places where the stitches cross. On the larger frames there is rather more scope for variation. The inner and outer circles can be worked in contrasting colours, and a third colour used to fill the hole with French knots. Instead of simply taking the thread over the edge, you can work buttonhole stitch. The photograph opposite will give you ideas for other interesting combinations and possibilities.

MAKING THE BUTTONS ON RINGS

1 Using a single strand of the green thread, work over the ring in buttonhole stitch.

2 Without fastening off, push the ridge towards the centre. Then work back and forth across the centre in two directions to form a network. Fasten off.

3 Work French knots in the chosen colours over the green threads, filling the centre completely. The underside of the knots will form a kind of shank, which can be sewn into when attaching the buttons.

MATERIALS

Blossom buttons

Plastic button frames in the chosen size(s)

Suitable embroidery thread, such as perlé cotton, soft (matte) embroidery cotton and/or 1.5mm ($\frac{1}{16}$ inch)-wide ribbon, in the chosen colours

Stranded cotton (floss) to match flower centre colour (see step 2)

Fine and medium-sized tapestry needles

Buttons on rings

Small metal rustproof rings; these can be found in hardware and craft shops and in haberdashery (notions) departments; they are intended for various purposes – not especially for buttons. Those shown are 12mm ($\frac{1}{2}$ inch) in diameter.

Perlé cotton in green and in 3 other colours

A medium-fine tapestry needle

FLOWER BED BUTTONS

These simple, yet effective buttons, reminiscent of small 'island' flower beds, consist of masses of tiny French knots covering an ordinary button form.

MAKING THE BUTTONS
1 If the buttons are intended to be washable, first wash the fabric to make sure that it is pre-shrunk.
2 Trace the ring shown here, and use this to mark and cut a template from the cardboard. Mark around the template on the fabric the required number of times, using an ordinary pencil.
3 Mount the fabric in an embroidery frame.
4 Using 2 strands of thread, and taking the thread twice around the needle , work 16 French knots in each colour. Scatter the knots randomly over the marked centre of each circle. Leave the two greens until last, and use these to fill any gaps.
5 Cut out the circles. Work gathering stitches around the edge of each circle.
6 Make up the button following the manufacturer's instructions, pulling up the gathering stitches once the embroidery has been correctly positioned.

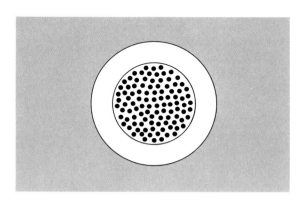

▲ Trace the ring and use it to cut out a cardboard template. Trace round the template on the fabric with a pencil the required number of times.

▼ The randomly scattered French knots in six colours (besides green) create an effect reminiscent of a well-stocked flower bed.

MATERIALS
Piece of lightweight plain-woven cotton large enough for the required number of buttons (see template above); cotton is easier to stretch over the button forms than synthetic fabric. The fabric will show through very slightly, so you should bear this in mind when choosing a colour.
Button forms for covering; the 15mm ($\frac{5}{8}$ inch) size aluminium forms made by Singer were used for these buttons.
Stranded cotton (floss) in 8 different colours; those used for the buttons shown are DMC 3340, 321, 996, 973, 552, 602, 704 and 700 (the last two are greens)
Fine crewel needle
Small piece of thin cardboard
Small piece of tracing paper
Sewing thread to match fabric

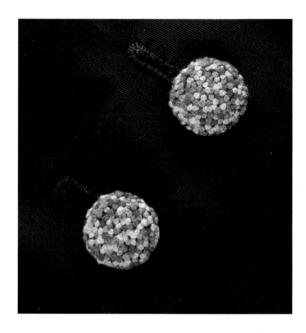

NOSEGAY BROOCHES

These little brooches are easy to make and can be co-ordinated with any outfit. Here, too, the foundation is a metal ring, and French knots provide an appealing texture.

MAKING THE BROOCHES

1 Cut a long length of thread – about 3 metres (10 feet) to avoid having to join the thread. Work around the ring in buttonhole stitch.

2 Without fastening off, push the ridge to the inside. Now work the stems. These should fan out more widely at the top than at the bottom. Begin by marking the centre of the bouquet – an appropriate distance to the right of the thread – with a pin. Similarly, mark the centre of the stems, just opposite the pin. Now take the thread slightly to the right of this point and work into one of the buttonhole knots. Then go back to the top edge and work into a knot slightly to the right of the thread. Continue in this way (having removed the marking pins), working clockwise, until the stems form a symmetrical shape. Fasten off.

3 Now work French knots over the fanned-out stems. Vary the size of the knots by using different thicknesses of thread or wrapping the thread more than once around the needle.

4 Using one strand of one of the flower colours, wrap this thread several times around the stems and tie it in a bow. Take the ends through the stems and fasten them on the underside.

5 Sew a safety pin to the back of the brooch.

6 Gently wash the brooch, then immerse it in a solution of starch. While it is still damp, shape the bows by inserting a knitting needle through each loop. Leave the brooch to dry.

MATERIALS

Metal rings, such as curtain rings; those used for the brooches shown measure about 4cm (1½ inch) in diameter
Perlé cotton in green
Glossy embroidery threads (perlé, stranded floss and/or coton à broder) in several colours for flowers
Medium-sized tapestry needle
Brass safety pins
Sewing thread for attaching pins
Laundry starch

Nosegay brooches are quite quick and easy to make. They can be colour co-ordinated with your wardrobe and would make a unique and charming present.

POSY NEEDLE BOOK

This little needle book, embroidered with a bouquet of roses, forget-me-nots and gypsophila, will keep your needles safe and organized. It would make a thoughtful gift for a friend or relative who sews or embroiders.

MAKING THE NEEDLE BOOK

1 From the blue fabric cut 4 pieces, each 11.5 by 9cm ($4\frac{1}{2}$ by $3\frac{1}{2}$ inches). Also cut 4 pieces of the interfacing, each 9 by 7cm ($3\frac{1}{2}$ by $2\frac{3}{4}$ inches).

2 Centre each piece of interfacing on a piece of fabric and iron it in place, following the manufacturer's instructions. Trim the fabric corners diagonally to reduce bulk; turn the edges to the wrong side and press them flat.

3 Using a single strand of the green coton à broder (shade 539), work blanket stitch around the edges of all four pieces. The stitches should be about 3–4mm (a generous $\frac{1}{8}$ inch) deep and 2–3mm ($\frac{1}{8}$ inch) apart.

4 Trace the pattern given below onto the tracing paper. Pin the tracing to one of the cover pieces.

5 Using a single strand of the white coton à broder, work backstitch in a zigzag pattern between the two circles. You may find it helpful to begin by working a wide, open machine zigzag stitch around the circle, then removing these stitches; this will leave a pattern of holes that can be followed when hand stitching.

MATERIALS

10cm ($\frac{1}{8}$ yard) of lightweight, closely woven blue evenweave linen or cotton

10cm ($\frac{1}{8}$ yard) of white evenweave fabric; the fabric used for this needle book has 28 threads to 2.5cm (1 inch)

10cm ($\frac{1}{8}$ yard) of medium-weight iron-on interfacing

DMC coton à broder, 1 skein each of the following colours: 539, 836 and white

DMC stranded cotton (floss), 1 skein each of the following colours: 601, 603 and 605

80cm ($\frac{7}{8}$ yard) of 1.5mm- ($\frac{1}{16}$ inch)-wide pink ribbon or no.3 perlé cotton

Medium-sized crewel needle

Piece of transfer adhesive or fusible web at least 7.5 by 18cm ($2\frac{3}{4}$ by 7 inches)

Small piece of tissue paper

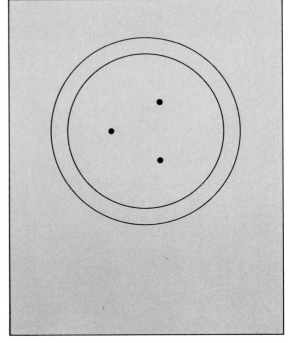

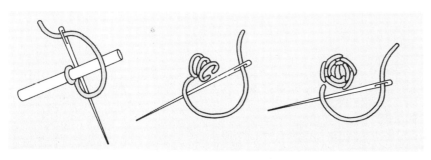

Rose stitch   Make 3 or 4 loops round a matchstick or pencil. Anchor them with a backstitch.

Work long loose stem stitches to encircle the loops and continue working round and round.

As you continue round, the stitches gradually become flatter so that the outside ones are lying flat.

6 Using all 6 strands of shade 605, work roses at the three points indicated, as shown in the rose stitch diagram opposite. Remove the tissue tracing.

7 Work a French knot, using 6 strands of 603, in the centre of each rose. Still using 603, work a few more, smaller roses, spacing them randomly. Work some French knot rosebuds in the same colour, and some more in 6 strands of 601.

8 Work the forget-me-nots in blue coton à broder (836) French knots and the gypsophila in white ones. Fill in the doily edges with more white French knots.

9 Fill in the spaces around the blossoms with green French knot 'leaves'.

10 Make two straight stitches with the narrow ribbon or perlé cotton for the bouquet ties.

11 Thread the ribbon or perlé cotton under the blanket stitches on all four cover pieces.

12 Using the transfer adhesive or fusible web, bond the front and back outer covers to the other two (inner cover) pieces. Oversew around all edges, using shade 539.

13 From the white evenweave, cut 4 pages, each 7.5 by 6cm (3 by 2½ inches). Work buttonhole stitch around all the edges, using shade 539.

14 Position the pages inside the covers, making sure that all the edges are aligned, to form the spine of the book. Using a single strand of 539, carefully oversew them together.

THE BIRDS AND THE BEES

I enjoy working in the garden on my own. The sense of seclusion and peace is comforting rather than lonely; but even when most absorbed in my work, I like to be aware of bird and insect life around me. Besides adding to the visual beauty of my surroundings, birds and bees bring a variety of sounds and a sense of purpose other than my own. We have all become aware of the need to attract and preserve wildlife; but even from a purely selfish point of view it makes sense to choose plants that have more to offer than just colour. A garden planted without consideration for the preferences of winged creatures often has an aimless, shallow character. Birds, bees and butterflies in my garden have given me as many unexpected moments of delight as the plants they settle on.

Butterflies and other insects

We humans tend to be subjective about wildlife, favouring furry or pretty creatures whose food preferences don't encroach on our own. For example, it is easy to arouse enthusiasm for protecting brilliantly coloured butterflies – not so easy in the case of the common white butterflies and their caterpillars, who feast on our cabbages, rapidly turning the leaves into lace curtains. It was one of these butterflies that served as inspiration for the handkerchief on page 103. The caterpillars sometimes spin their cocoons on the walls of my workroom and pupate there during the winter. Late one January night, I glanced up from my embroidery to behold the astonishing sight of a newly emerged white butterfly fluttering over my head.

It is possible, I have found, to enjoy the delicate beauty of these butterflies without sacrificing your cabbages. Given a choice, the caterpillars seem to like nasturtiums just as much. If you train the flowers up canes, the butterflies will come to them first and lay their eggs on the nasturtium leaves. When the leaves are thoroughly infested, you can uproot the plants and discard them.

Such lowly creatures as ants and aphids, worms and woodlice can be merely a nuisance or a real pest, depending on where you live and what you grow. Nevertheless, they give the garden a life of its own, and I control them reluctantly and as harmlessly as I can. Even the despised slugs and snails have their own appeal (and snails have always been a favourite subject for embroiderers).

Birds

Birds, too, can be destructive, but I forgive them because I enjoy their company. Some are even beneficial to the gardener, feeding on pests. I have had to protect them from my cat by tagging him with an enormous bell to give them advance warning.

I used to go to great trouble protecting our beautiful fan-trained redcurrant bush from the blackbirds. I would net the bush to keep

Both the birds (and the nest) in this charming engraving could be traced and used as an embroidery design either in combination or as separate motifs.

the birds off the fruit; and when the berries were ripe, I would harvest them and weigh them proudly. After that, all was anti-climax, for no one in my family really likes redcurrants, and finding a use for them was a bit of a chore. Now, we simply relax and enjoy the sight of the blackbirds stripping the fruit from the bush. The glossy black feathers against the glowing, translucent red berries and fresh green leaves is a splendid sight – one that would make a lovely design for embroidery.

For the embroidered cushion shown on page 105, however, I decided against representing a particular, or even symbolic, bird – choosing, rather, to convey in a more stylized way what birds in general mean to me as a gardener and as an embroiderer. The birds that visit my garden have a special significance for me because they have chosen to come into my world. In a garden, where one tries to have everything planned and under control, the element of surprise is often missing. Birds can provide this with a sudden flash of colour or a flurry of movement, or by the brightness and cheerfulness of their song.

It is a special joy to come across an occupied nest. The hatching of eggs and the development of young broods reinforces the feeling of new life and growth in the garden during spring and summer. Even a dropped feather is a small treasure. Because of their structure and range of colouring, feathers are fascinating in themselves, and they have often been used as the basis of needlework designs. For the cushion, I have arranged

With their lacy wings and striped bodies, bees, singly or in groups, make perfect motifs for embroidery. Gardeners rely on them for pollination, as do bee-keepers for honey, and what would summer be without their hum?

them in a spiral pattern to suggest movement and flight as well as the shape of the nest, with its precious eggs.

The perfection of form exemplified by eggs and feathers is found also in the honeycomb, whose hexagonal cavities have traditionally inspired one of the most popular forms of patchwork. For the cushion on page 97 I have chosen to interpret this motif literally, in honey-coloured satin, complete with grains of yellow pollen and a portrait of a honey bee. The industrious character of these appealing insects can serve as a model for the embroiderer and gardener alike!

A good way to use butterflies in embroidery is with their wings spread (rather than in profile), so that the symmetry of the pattern and the jewel-like colours are fully revealed.

Honeycomb Cushion

The play of light on this honeycomb patchwork is achieved simply by using a satin-weave fabric and turning the patches to lie in different directions.

MAKING THE PATCHWORK

1 Prepare the fabric, if necessary (see page 139). Trace the smaller of the two concentric hexagons, and use this tracing to make a template from thin cardboard, taking care to cut accurately. Use this template to cut out 39 hexagons from the writing paper. Be accurate, or your patchwork will not join up properly.

2 Trace the larger hexagon and make another template to this size. Use this to mark and cut 39 hexagons from fabric.

3 Centre a paper hexagon on the wrong side of a fabric hexagon, and fold the edges over it carefully to give an even seam allowance all around. Tack (baste) this turning in place, through the paper, taking care to fold the corners neatly. Continue until you have 39 hexagons backed with paper.

4 Now assemble the hexagons into strips. Place two

MATERIALS

I metre (I yard) of honey-coloured
  satin-weave fabric, 90cm (36 inches)
  wide; the fabric should take a crease
  well and not fray easily
OR 10 metres (11 yards) of satin
  ribbon, at least 7cm (2¾ inches) wide
Small piece of evenweave cotton or
  linen fabric with 22–25 threads to
  2.5cm (I inch)
DMC stranded cotton (floss), I skein
  each of the following colours: 3371,
  783, 785, 945
Very fine medium-brown thread, such
  as silk machine embroidery thread
  or that used for mending stockings

Sewing thread to match fabric
Crewel needle, size 9 or 10
Cushion pad (pillow form) 35cm
  (14 inches) square
Zip fastener, 30cm (12 inches) long
  (optional)
Tracing paper
Several sheets of writing paper or
  other fairly stiff paper
Small piece of thin cardboard
Tissue paper
Set square (right-angled triangle)

Size of finished cushion: approximately
  35cm (14 inches) square, excluding
  trim.

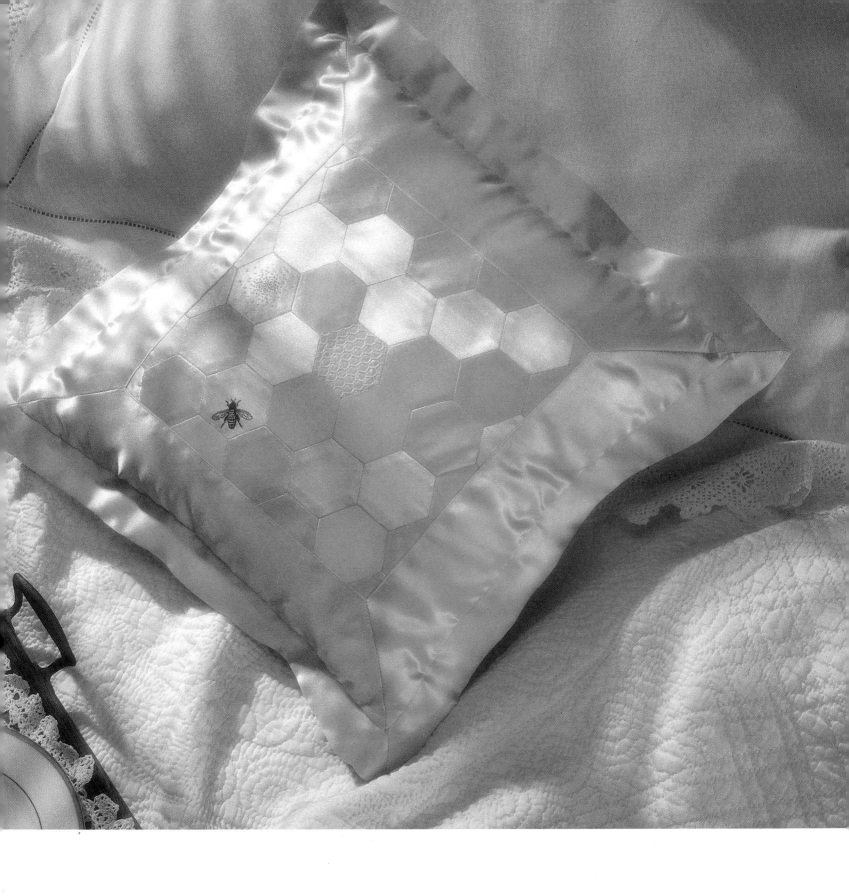

patches together with right sides facing, making sure that the edges and corners line up exactly and that the direction of the weave is different. Oversew the two edges to be joined, using tiny stitches. Repeat, adding another patch to the opposite edge of one of the hexagons. Continue in this way, to make 4 strips of 6 patches each and 3 strips of 5. Make sure to vary the weave direction.

5 Join the strips to form a rectangle.

WORKING THE EMBROIDERY

1 Note the position of the hexagon on which the bee is embroidered (see photograph), and remove the tacking (basting) stitches and backing paper from this hexagon.

2 Trace the bee design onto tissue paper, using a very hard pencil. Tack (baste) the tracing to the hexagon, positioning the bee as shown.

3 Using one strand of shade 3371 and working in split stitch, outline the body and put in the legs and antennae. (You may find it easier to work the embroidery if you first mount a piece of lawn in a small ring frame, then tack [baste] the patch over this. Work the embroidery through both layers, then trim away the excess lawn afterwards.)

Trace the two concentric hexagons to make two cardboard templates. Trace the bee (actual size). Tack (baste) the tracing to a hexagon as shown.

4 Now work the wings, using very fine brown thread (a long hair can be used, if you cannot find suitable thread), and working in split stitch (or small backstitches if using a hair). Outline the wings first, then fill in the veins.

5 Carefully tear away the tissue paper. Fill in the head and thorax in 3371, using satin stitch, and work a French knot for each eye.

6 Work the stripes as follows. Still using one strand of 3371, work buttonhole stitches across the fourth segment from the top. The solid edge of the stitching should lie towards the sting, and there

This close-up photograph of the cushion shows details of the embroidery: the honeycomb (steps 8 and 9), the pollen grains (step 7), and the bee (steps 1 to 6). Position the three embroidered hexagons in relation to each other as shown here.

should be about a one-thread space between the stitches. Repeat on the next three segments. Using one strand of shade 783, work 2 or 3 straight stitches across the top segment of the abdomen. Work buttonhole stitch across the remaining segments.

7 Remove the backing paper from the pollen hexagon, and work the pollen in French knots, using one strand of 725 and scattering the knots as shown.

8 Remove the backing paper from the honeycomb hexagon. Tack (baste) the piece of evenweave fabric just outside the edge of the hexagon, and then work straight stitches as shown in Diagram A, using 2 strands of shade 945. The stitches are arranged in a staggered pattern; each stitch crosses 5 threads, and there are 6 vertical threads between stitches and one horizontal thread separating the rows.

9 When all the vertical stitches are in place, thread 2 strands of 945 through the stitches as shown in the diagram. Take the thread through to the back of the fabric at the end of each row. Check that the pattern is complete, and then carefully pull out all the threads of the evenweave fabric.

MAKING THE BORDER AND TRIM

1 Draw a trapezium-shaped (trapezoid-shaped) pattern for the border, as follows. Rule a line 21cm (8¾ inches) long. Rule a line down at right angles from each end and measure off 6.5cm (2½ inches) to make three sides of a rectangle. Draw the fourth side, extending the base line at least 10cm (4 inches)

at each end. Place a set square (right-angled triangle) on one top corner of the rectangle and measure an angle of 45°. Rule a line through this point to meet the extended line at the base of the rectangle. Repeat at the other side to make a trapezium (trapezoid). Measure a seam allowance of 1.5cm (⅝ inch) all round. If you are using ribbon, omit the upper and lower seam allowances. Use the pattern to cut 4 border pieces from the fabric or ribbon.

2 Stitch the strips together along their diagonal edges. (If using fabric, first turn under and press the upper seam allowance.) Press the seams open.

3 Pin and tack (baste) the border in place. Topstitch close to the edge. Trim off the excess patchwork and neaten the edge with oversewing or zigzag stitch. Carefully remove the tacking (basting) stitches from the patchwork, then press the work from the wrong side. Finally, remove the papers.

4 Make a pattern for the mitred trim, as follows. Measure the length of one border strip along its outer edge. (If you have used fabric, measure *along the seamline – not* the raw edge.) This will be called 'measurement x'. Add 11cm (4½ inches) to measurement x, and cut a strip of paper to this length, 9cm (3½ inches) wide. Mark 1.5cm (⅝ inch) seam allowances on both long edges. Mark the centre point of the strip, and measure out from this point, along the upper seamline, one-half of measurement x; mark this point (see diagram overleaf). Fold the strip in half lengthwise. Using a set square (right-angled triangle), draw a 45° angle from the folded edge through this point. Draw another line, parallel to it, 1.5cm (⅝ inch) outside it; this marks the seam allowance. Cut along this outer line through both thicknesses of the paper. Finally, unfold the strip and re-fold it widthwise through the centre point. Using the previously shaped end as a pattern, trim the other end to match.

5 Use this pattern to cut 4 border strips from the fabric. If you are using ribbon, centre the ribbon under the pattern so that the seam allowances, though narrower, will be even.

6 Stitch the strips together with right sides facing; trim the seam allowances at the points; press the seams open and turn the trim right side out. Tack (baste) the raw edges together and press the fold.

Work the honeycomb embroidery on a piece of evenweave fabric in staggered vertical stitches (step 8). Then thread through the vertical in a zig-zag pattern (step 9). When the honeycomb is complete, carefully pull out all the threads of the evenweave fabric.

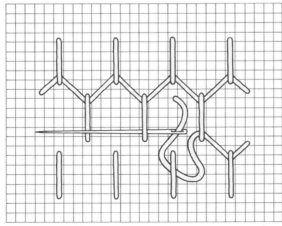

MAKING UP THE CUSHION

1 Measure the front cover and cut a piece of fabric the same size for the back.

1a If you are using ribbon, cut 10 lengths to this measurement. Weave the strips in a chequerboard effect to make up the required area. Tack (baste) the ribbons in place, and secure them with small running stitches close to the edges, as shown in the photograph.

2 Tack (baste) the trim to the right side of the front cover with raw edges matching. Make up the cover as described on page 141, including a zip fastener, if desired, in one seam.

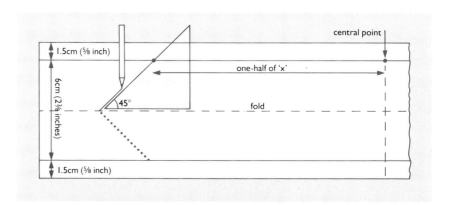

Make a pattern for the mitred trim, following the instructions in step 4 on the previous page.

If you are using ribbon to make the back of the cushion, weave 10 lengths, cut to the same size as the front cover, to make a chequerboard effect. Secure them with small running stitches close to the edges as shown in this detail.

BUTTERFLY HANDKERCHIEF

This cabbage white butterfly spreads its wings against a lacy pulled-thread background which suggests a cabbage leaf after a visit from some hungry caterpillars.

WORKING THE EMBROIDERY

1 Mount the handkerchief in the frame, but not too tightly. If using a slate frame, sew it to the tapes through the hem; if using a ring frame, tack (baste) strips of fabric along two adjacent sides, so that one corner will lie within the ring.

2 Using the water-erasable pen, mark a point about 10cm (4 inches) from one corner along two adjacent sides. Then, using a ruler as a guide, mark a straight line between these two points.

3 Using a single strand of the floss, work along this line in backstitch. Then work open stem stitches just outside this line of backstitch and along the other two sides of the triangle. Make the stitches about 2 mm ($\frac{1}{8}$ inch) long, and slant them (see stitch diagram overleaf).

4 Trace the outline of the butterfly (omitting the antennae) onto tissue paper, and tack (baste) the tracing to the fabric, using small running stitches and contrasting thread; then gently tear the tracing away.

5 Now work punch stitch (also known as mock faggot filling) all over the triangular area, as shown. Use a single strand of the floss and the tapestry needle, and work all the vertical stitches first, then work the horizontal stitches back over them.

6 Next, work the outline of the butterfly in split stitch, still using one strand of the cotton floss, and removing the running stitches as you go.

7 Work the dots on the wings in tiny backstitches,

in a circle; work the wing tip markings in running stitch.

8 Work the body in padded satin stitch, using 2 strands.

9 Put in the antennae by eye; first lay a single thread of mending cotton or button thread on the fabric and couch it in place with tiny stitches, using a single

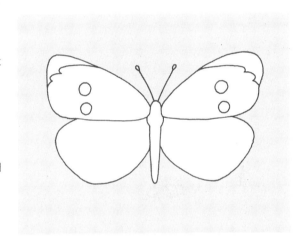

Trace the outline of the butterfly onto tissue paper and then tack (baste) the tracing to the fabric, using small running stitches and contrasting thread. Carefully tear away the tracing paper. It is not necessary to trace the antennae, but they are included here as a guide for positioning.

MATERIALS

Plain white linen handkerchief, at least 28cm (11 inches) square; make sure it is evenweave, with at least 40 threads to 2.5cm (1 inch)
White stranded embroidery cotton (floss), 1 skein
White mercerized cotton
White mending cotton or button thread
Tapestry needle, size 25 or 26
Crewel needle, size 9 or 10
Slate frame or ring frame
Water-erasable pen
Tissue paper

strand of the floss. Then, without fastening off, work back over the thread, covering it with close whip stitches, to make the antenna stand out. Work the other antenna in the same way.

10 Remove the handkerchief from the frame; wash it carefully (making sure that all traces of the marking pen are removed), and starch it. Stretch it gently into shape, and press it firmly, but carefully, from the wrong side, into a thick soft pad.

Open stem stitch The method of working is basically the same as ordinary stem stitch, but the stitches are worked at a 45° angle to the line, and a very small space should be left between the stitches.

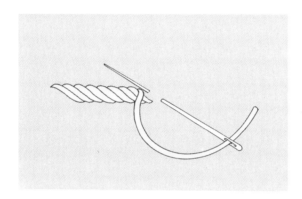

Punch stitch (mock faggot filling) This is worked over 4 fabric threads in each direction. Begin with rows of vertical stitches, working them in pairs and working them into the same holes. Pull the stitches to draw the fabric threads together. Then work pairs of back stitches horizontally, again pulling the stitches.

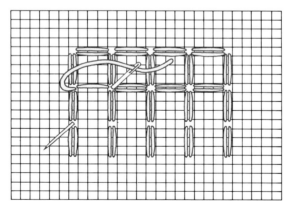

FEATHER CUSHION

*The wonderful diversity of birds' eggs and
feathers is suggested on this cushion by
using different counted thread stitches.*

PREPARING THE FABRIC
1 Cut a piece of fabric 48cm (19 inches) wide from
one end of the piece. Prepare it as appropriate (see
page 139). Find the centre point, and mark it
temporarily with a pin.
2 Place the fabric on a board, or other flat working
surface, and tape or weight it in place. Improvise a
compass from a drawing pin (thumbtack), a piece of
string and a water-erasable marker pen, adjusting
the string so that it measures 23cm (9 inches)
between pen and pin. Put the drawing pin at the
centre of the fabric, and mark a circle of 23cm
(9 inches) radius.

MATERIALS
60cm (⅝ yard) of 122cm- (48 inch-) wide
   evenweave ecru linen with 35 threads to 2.5cm
   (1 inch)
DMC coton à broder, 4 skeins of shade 415
DMC stranded cotton (floss), 1 skein of
   shade 747
Stranded cotton (floss), 1 skein of a shade to
   match fabric
Danish Flower Thread; 1 skein of shade HF 222,
   OR DMC coton à broder, shade 644
Tapestry needle, size 24
Fine crewel needle
Slate frame, or rectangular frame
Tracing paper
Embroidery transfer pencil, or dressmaker's
   carbon
Water-erasable pen
Round (preferably feather-filled) cushion pad
   (pillow form) 45cm (18 inches) in diameter

Size of finished cushion: 43cm (17 inches) in
   diameter, excluding frill.

3 Zigzag stitch around the inside of the circle to reinforce it, but do not cut it out. Make a 5 mm ($\frac{1}{4}$ inch) hem on the edges of the fabric, and stitch it in place with a row of zigzag. (This step can be omitted if you are using a simple rectangular frame.) Mark the vertical and horizontal centres with running stitches, following the fabric threads.

4 Frame up the fabric in a slate frame, or mount it on a rectangular frame. Do not stretch it too tightly, because it will not be under tension when finished; it should be just taut enough to expose the weave.

5 Enlarge the design (see page 109) as instructed. Trace the enlarged design, including the centre point and the mark indicating the top. Transfer the design to the fabric, using either dressmaker's carbon or an embroidery transfer pencil (first test

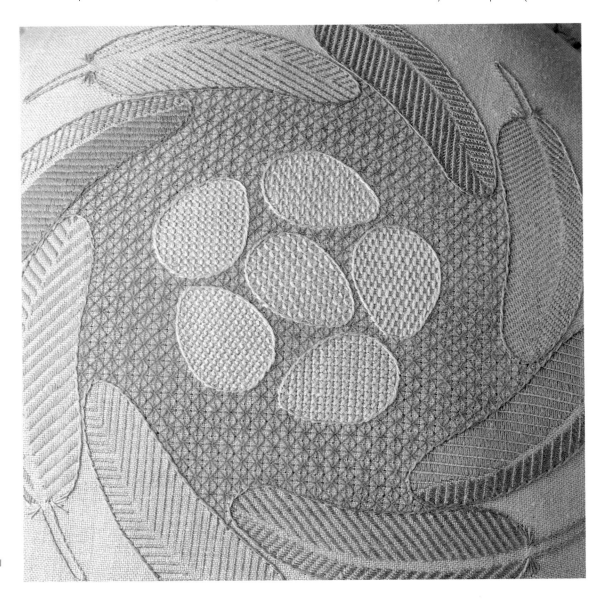

The 'nest' – the mossy background – is worked in Algerian eye stitch over 8 threads. Be careful not to pull the stitches tight.

the tranfer pencil on a spare piece of fabric to make sure it does not smudge). Align the 'top' mark and centre point of the design with these corresponding points on the fabric.

WORKING THE EMBROIDERY

1 Using a single strand of coton à broder, shade 415, work the feathers according to the diagram on page 108. First outline each feather in stem stitch, the quills in split stitch. Work a few straight stitches at the base of the feather. Then work the patterns using the tapestry needle; all of the feathers are darned except for feather B, which is worked in rows of satin stitch.

2 Work the eggs according to the diagram on page 109, using stranded floss, shade 747. First outline the eggs in stem stitch, using 2 strands of the thread. Then, using the tapestry needle, work the patterns as indicated. Use 2 strands for eggs 1 and 2; 3 strands for the others.

3 Work the mossy background in Danish Flower Thread (or similar matt-finish thread), using one strand in the tapestry needle. The stitch used, Algerian eye, is shown on page 41; but for this design it is worked over 8 fabric threads, not 4. Do not pull the stitches tight, as when forming eyelets.

MAKING UP THE CUSHION

1 Remove the fabric from the frame, and wash and press it. Cut out the circle just outside the reinforcing stitching.

2 Use the embroidered circle as a pattern to mark another circle for the back of the cushion. Reinforce this circle with zigzag stitch, and cut it out.

3 From the remaining fabric cut 4 strips, 6.5cm ($2\frac{1}{2}$ inches) wide and 56cm (22 inches) long, cutting along a fabric thread.

4 Measure in 1.5cm ($\frac{5}{8}$ inch) from one long edge on each strip; withdraw 4 threads beginning at this measurement. Turn up and tack (baste) a double hem. Using a single strand of the matching stranded floss and the tapestry needle, work hemstitching as shown, grouping 4 vertical threads with each stitch.

5 Join the strips to form a ring, using neat lapped or French seams.

6 Using the coton à broder, shade 415, work feather stitch about 1cm ($\frac{3}{8}$ inch) from the top of the hemstitching.

7 Work a row of gathering stitches along the other edge of the frill. Pin the frill to the front of the cushion cover with right sides facing, and pull up the gathering thread to fit the cover, adjusting the gathers evenly. Tack (baste) and stitch the frill in place.

8 Turn under 1cm ($\frac{3}{8}$ inch) along part of the edge of the back cover, for a distance of about 33cm (13 inches). Machine stitch this hem in place.

9 Place the front and back covers together, right sides facing, with the frill sandwiched between them. Tack (baste) and machine stitch them together, taking a 1cm ($\frac{3}{8}$ inch) seam allowance and reinforcing the points next to the hem.

10 Turn the cover right side out, and insert the cushion pad. Close the gap with hand stitches, which can be unpicked when the cover needs washing.

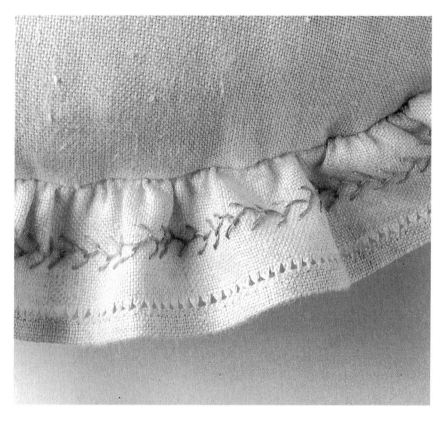

Detail showing the hemstitch and feather stitch border. The hemstitching is completed before the border strips are joined (with neat lapped or French seams); the feather stitching afterwards. The border is then gathered to make a frill and attached to the cushion.

Outline the feathers and eggs in stem stitch and then work them individually as shown on this page (feathers) and opposite (eggs).

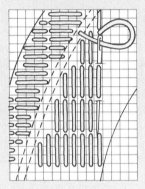

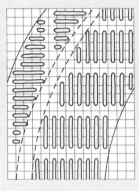

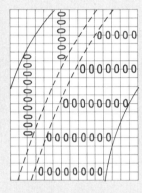

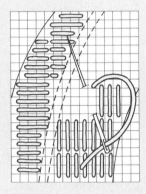

Feather a This is worked in double darning, over and under 4 threads, then returning over the row just worked, covering the threads left uncovered on the first journey.

Feather b Darn over 4 threads and under 1.

Feather c Darn over 1 thread and under 3.

Feather d This is worked in rows of satin stich, over 4 threads.

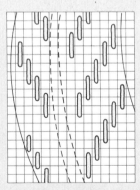

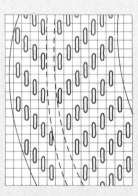

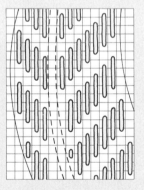

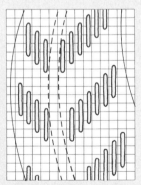

Feather e This pattern is worked diagonally, darning over 3 threads and under 6, and each stitch, moving outward from the midrib, moves up 2 fabric threads from the previous one.

Feather f Darn over 2 and under 2, moving up 1 fabric thread as you work out from the midrib.

Feather g Darn over 4 and under 2, moving up 1 fabric thread as you work outwards.

Feather h Darn over 4 and under 4, moving up 1 fabric thread as you work outwards.

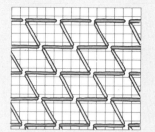

Egg 1 First work lines of backstitch, spaced 3 fabric threads apart, working over 4 threads for each stitch and moving 2 vertical threads to the right for each row; these stitches are shown in black. Then work diagonal lines of backstitch (blue stitches) across the first lines.

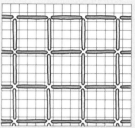

Egg 2 First work horizontal lines of backstitch over 4 threads, spacing the lines 4 threads apart (black stitches). Then work vertical lines of backstitch (blue) to form the square pattern.

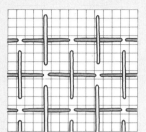

Egg 3 First work backstitch over 6 fabric threads, spacing the rows 4 threads apart (black stitches) and staggering them as shown. Then work darning stitches (blue) across these stitches, going over 6 threads and under 2.

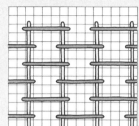

Egg 4 First work darning stitches over 6 fabric threads and under 2, spacing the rows 2 threads apart and staggering them as shown (black stitches). Then thread another strand of thread (blue) under these stitches where they overlap.

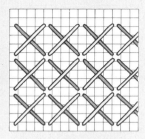

Egg 5 Work cross stitch over 4 fabric threads.

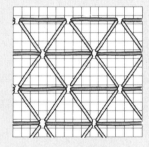

Egg 6 First work backstitches over 6 fabric threads, spacing the rows 4 fabric threads apart and staggering them as shown (black stitches). Then work diagonal lines of backstitch (blue) across these stitches as shown.

TOP

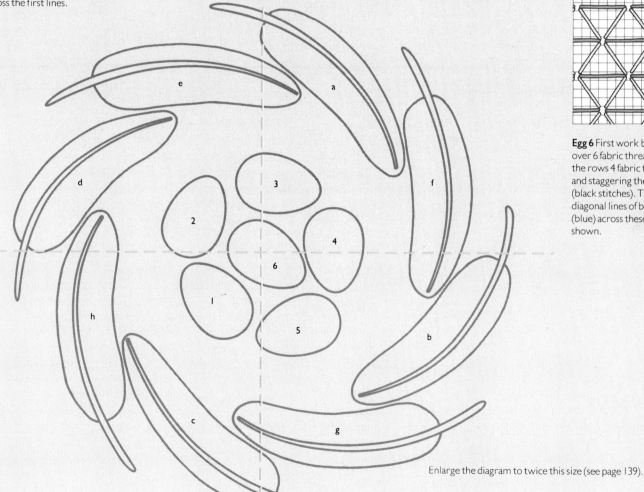

Enlarge the diagram to twice this size (see page 139).

WONDERFUL WEEDS

Along with the increasing respect today for herbs and wildflowers has come the realization that most weeds are so considered only because they are gate-crashers in our gardens. In other habitats their virtues might be more apparent to us, and although weeds are a nuisance for all gardeners, perhaps we should not let that blind us to their beauties.

For the purposes of this book, I would define as a garden weed any plant that threatens others by its over-zealous colonization, or that is such a shy performer that it might not deserve the space it occupies. Similarly unwelcome are those plants that persistently disrupt the smooth uniformity of our lawns; conversely, grass itself can be a weed when it invades paved or cobbled areas.

More than cultivated forms of plants – many of which will die or fail to thrive if conditions don't suit them – weeds are capable of adapting to their surroundings. They exhibit varying forms and habits, from stunted starveling to lush invader, in response to the available moisture and nourishment.

My approach to weeds is the labour-intensive one of weeding by hand, rather than the easier option of weedkillers. I cannot claim that this is primarily from a virtuous desire to avoid using pollutants – although that is a factor. Rather, it is because many of the places in my garden that are inhabited by weeds have also been colonized by self-sown seedlings of desirable plants, which would be wiped out, along with the weeds, if I were to apply a weedkiller. I must admit that I rather enjoy weeding; especially after rain, it can be therapeutic and satisfying.

So long as they are not allowed to over-indulge their invasive tendencies, some weeds can complement more carefully chosen plants, and their appearance in unexpected places need not be totally discouraged. Except in a very formal garden, a lawn sprinkled with daisies and clover can be much prettier than a plain expanse of close-cut green. The next time you do uproot these weeds, have a good look at them; they have much of the charm of the old illustrated herbals (such as those overleaf) in which they were often depicted, and which can provide designs for embroidery. A plantain, for instance, has leaves with a pronounced 'quilted' pattern (rather like a hosta). Its flower spike has a neatly textured pattern of overlapping scales which could be suggested by fly stitch or French knots.

Because I don't use weedkillers on it, my cobbled path supports a variety of self-seeded plants, including many things I might not have thought of planting there, even if I had been able to find a way of introducing the seedlings into the tiny gaps between the cobbles. There are little cushions of moss, mats of creeping thyme, forget-me-nots, daisies, *Arenaria balearica* (sandwort), creeping mint and a well-grown bush of lemon balm, as well as the ubiquitous plantains and dandelions, forced into tidiness by the limitations of this habitat.

Dandelions

The dandelion is a common weed of wide distribution, occurring in more than a hundred species. It causes gardeners plenty of problems, and yet it has a long and honourable history as a plant with many uses for humans. All parts of the dandelion are useful medicinally, and it does not become toxic when taken in quantity, as some medicinal

The neat buds, the sunny, yellow flowerheads and the feathery parachutes of the dandelion 'clock' are all ideal subjects for needlework designs. They can be used as single motifs or to form a regular or random pattern.

plants do. In addition, each part of the plant has other practical uses: the leaf in salads, the flower in wine-making, the dried root as a coffee substitute and the milky latex contained in the tubular stem as a source of rubber.

I am usually too busy trying to control the dandelions in my garden to admire their beauty, but beautiful they are, and interesting too, especially when examined in detail. The tightly closed flower bud bursts open into the cheerful, sunny yellow flower, whose strap-shaped petals can be well suggested by embroidering them in very narrow yellow ribbon. When the flower is past its best it closes up again to allow the seed heads to develop, and then the bud bursts a second time, opening out into the characteristic feathery sphere, beloved of children and a source of simple rituals involving blowing and counting. For the embroidery on the blouse shown on page 115, I used this seed motif, positioning it formally on the collar and front band and suggesting the flight of the seeds on the pocket.

Daises

The daisy is much less of a problem than the dandelion because its roots are fibrous and more easily removed, and it is not such a prolific seeder. The common daisy is often overlooked, now that there are so many larger-flowered and brightly coloured versions available. To me, these modern cultivars seem coarse and unbalanced beside the original, and in bad weather they look like old mops, whereas the flowers of the true daisy remain pristine throughout heavy rain and hard frosts. This is due mainly to their ability to close in poor light and at night. One of the daisy's relatives, *Bellium minutum*, is a miniature version of the common daisy and a lovely plant to have growing in the cracks between paving stones.

As well as being decorative, daisy chains for me are a symbol of a carefree childhood, which is why I used one as a border for the central medallion of a daisy plant in the embroidered picture shown on page 111. Because daisies bloom in England almost throughout the year, I wanted to use the petals and yellow centres of the flowers to symbolize the passage of time. For this reason, there are four quarter flowers representing the four astronomical quarters of the year and four circles of yellow disc florets symbolizing the four seasons. The petals are divided into sets of seven, giving the days of the week, and there are twelve daisies in the daisy chain, giving the months in the year.

The daisy has an even greater affinity with the sun than the dandelion (which opens in daylight and closes in darkness). It responds even more precisely to the amount of light available by the degree to which it opens or closes its petals, and in addition, the flower turns in the direction of the sun. This is the reason for the four square daisies, one at each corner, which suggest, in the spread of their petals, a sunburst motif.

The scarlet pimpernel
A third weed that shares this response to sunlight is the scarlet pimpernel (*Anagallis arvensis*). It is rather misnamed, since its flowers can also be blue, but it is rather an elegant plant, and a pleasure to discover in the garden. I think it's very suitable for an embroidery design (such as the collar shown on page 119), because it's one of those flowers with sepals visible between the petals, which gives it a formal aspect. It also has interesting seed capsules, which look like small peas. When ripe, each capsule splits around the middle to disperse the seed, leaving one half attached to the flower stem like a fairy cap.

As an annual whose restrained growth does not threaten other plants, the pimpernel falls into the category of plants that are so insignificant that most people would never think of planting them. However, once seen it's hard to forget, and I have left my plant to seed itself in the hope that others will appear elsewhere in the garden.

Unpopular with those who want a fine lawn, the plantain is nevertheless a gift for embroidery design. Its form and texture are perfect for interpreting in needlework.

DANDELION BLOUSE

Motifs based on the little parachute seeds dispersed from the dandelion flower decorate the collar and centre front band of this blouse and fly across the pocket as if blown by the wind. The motif can easily be adapted to any similar blouse pattern.

EMBROIDERING THE BLOUSE

Note It is usually best to work embroidery before cutting out the garment piece(s), so you may wish to mark the cutting lines of the relevant pieces on the fabric with dressmaker's carbon, work the embroidery (in a frame, if you prefer), then cut out the pieces.

1 If the pattern has a fly front opening, as this one does, trace the vertical sequence of motifs given on page 116, repeating it as required to extend down the opening. Also mark the centre front on the tracing. Tack (baste) the tracing to the fabric, centring it carefully.

2 If the pattern has no pocket and you wish to add one, you can use the pattern provided, tracing the motifs at the same time. Otherwise, you can adapt the pattern and the motifs to suit yourself. Or you can adapt the motifs to suit an existing pocket pattern. In any case, the complete design should be traced and the embroidery worked through the tracing.

3 Similarly, the three seed motif can be used as is on

MATERIALS
Blouse pattern with collar
Fabric, buttons, thread, etc., as required
Stranded cotton to contrast or harmonize with
  fabric; the shade used here is DMC 676
Fine crewel needle
Ring frame (optional)
Lightweight tracing or tissue paper
Dressmaker's carbon paper (optional)

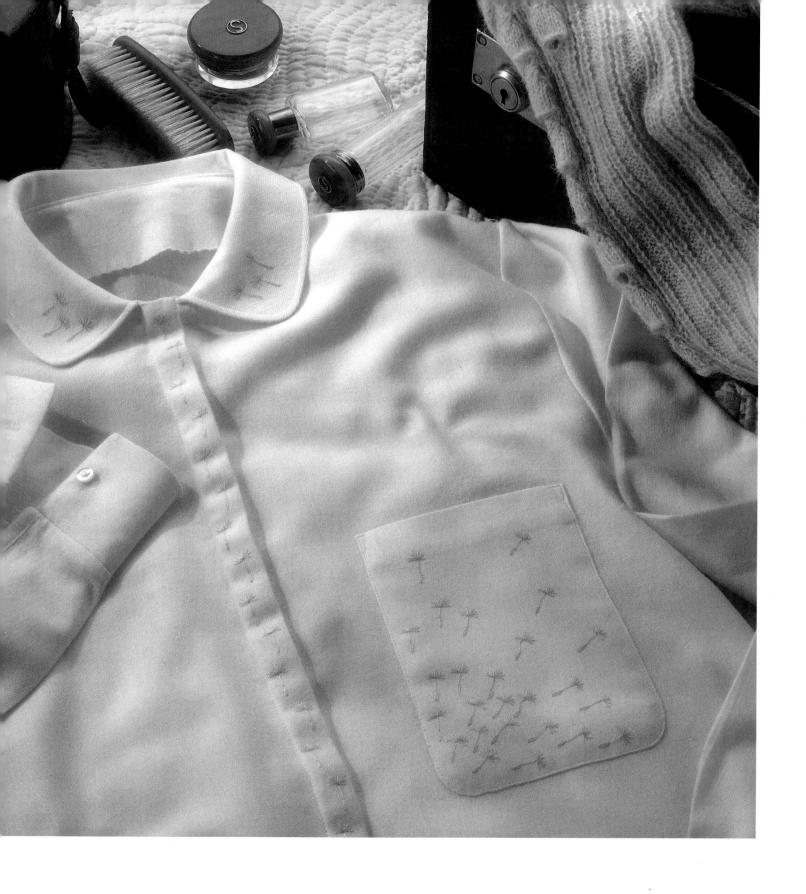

the collar, or adapted to suit the individual blouse pattern. On the back of this collar are two individual seed motifs.

4 Using a single strand of the floss, work the motifs as follows: for the seed itself, work a detached chain stitch, then work a straight stitch inside it; then work a single straight stitch joining the seed to the feathery part; for the latter, work short straight stitches, taking each one down into the same central hole. Anchor the thread on the underside before taking it on to the next motif; where seeds are separated by more than about 1 cm ($\frac{1}{2}$ inch), fasten off and then fasten on for the next, to prevent the thread from pulling between them.

5 Press the work from the wrong side. Make up the blouse as instructed by the pattern.

centre front

▲ Trace the three seed motifs (actual size) for positioning on the front of the collar. The motifs can be easily adapted to use singly or in other combinations.

▶ For embroidering a fly front opening, trace the sequence of motifs (actual size), repeating it until the tracing is the required length.

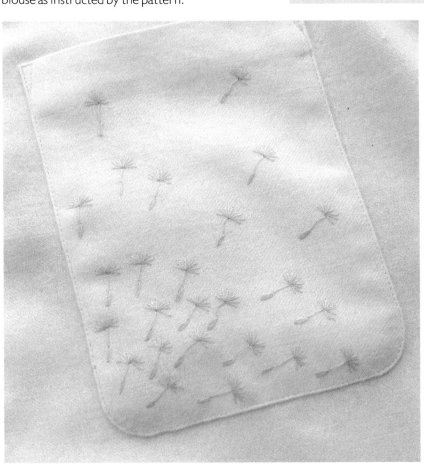

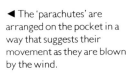

◀ The 'parachutes' are arranged on the pocket in a way that suggests their movement as they are blown by the wind.

fold and stitch

fold here

seam allowance

To make the pocket, trace the cutting, stitching and fold lines and the embroidery design. To adapt the design for a different pocket, simply trace the design and then adjust to fit the individual blouse pattern.

Scarlet Pimpernel Collar

Delicate flowers of the scarlet pimpernel adorn this simple collar – a versatile accessory for a round-necked blouse, dress or pullover. The collar can be made either in one piece or in two, for use on a back-fastening garment. It is catch-stitched to the neckline so that it can be removed for washing.

PREPARING THE FABRIC

1 Prepare the fabric as appropriate (see page 139).
2 Trace the collar pattern, given full-size on page 120. Before cutting out the tracing, check the inner neck measurement (twice measurement A) against the neckline of the garment, and extended or shorten the pattern at the foldline if necessary.
3 If you wish to make the collar for a back-opening garment, eliminate the foldline and re-shape that edge as desired (see the diagram on page 121), drawing a curved shape or a pointed one, as desired, and adding 1cm ($\frac{3}{8}$ inch) seam allowance.
4 Cut out the pattern. Cut it twice from the main fabric (or four times, if the collar is to be divided), placing it on the fold/lengthwise grain of the fabric. Cut out the collar pieces.
5 Trim about 4mm (generous $\frac{1}{8}$ inch) from the pattern, excluding the foldline. Use this pattern to cut 2 pieces from the interfacing.
6 Iron each interfacing piece to a collar section, leaving an even margin all round.
7 Trace the pimpernel motif, including the point of the collar for positioning, using a pen. Tape this to a window with sunlight behind it. Tape one of the collar sections over the motif, aligning the edges with the traced collar point, and trace the motif, using a hard black pencil. Trace the motif onto the other point of the collar.
8 The interfacing makes the fabric quite stiff, and you may find it convenient to work the embroidery in the hand. If not, tack (baste) it to a piece of lawn mounted in a ring frame. Cut away the lawn underneath the motif. When the embroidery is complete, remove the tacking.

WORKING THE EMBROIDERY

Note All of the embroidery except the flower centres is worked in a single strand of the floss.
1 For the flower petals (scarlet), first work one detached chain stitch down the centre of each petal to give a slight padding. Then cover this with satin stitch, worked sideways across the detached chain.
2 For the sepals, work detached chain stitches in medium apple green, twisting the stitch twice before anchoring it.
3 Work the flower centres in French knots, using 2 strands of the floss and anchoring each knot twice to flatten it.

MATERIALS

30cm ($\frac{1}{4}$ yard) of fine white cotton or
   linen lawn or cambric
Small amount of fine, soft, non-woven
   iron-on interfacing
Stranded embroidery cotton (floss) in
   deep wine red, scarlet, and medium
   and pale apple green; the shades used
   are DMC 3685, 350, 3347 and 3348

Scrap of fine white fabric for neckband
   (see step 5 of 'Making up the Collar')
Fine crewel needle
Small ring frame (optional)
Two pieces of lawn to fit frame
   (optional)
Good quality tracing paper
Masking tape
Hard black pencil

foldline

lengthwise grain of fabric

4 Work the stems in pale apple green; the main stem in wide stem stitch and the flower stems in ordinary stem stitch.

5 Work the buds in the medium green and the scarlet, using satin stitch and letting the colours encroach on each other where they meet, to show how the long sepals enclose the petals.

6 Work the leaves in the medium green, using buttonhole stitch, with the ridge forming the outline of the leaf and with the longer legs of the stitch slanting towards the centre to indicate the veins each side of the midrib.

measurement A

stitch line

Trace the pattern and design (actual size). Before cutting it out, check that inner neck fits the garment (twice Measurement A). Shorten or lengthen at the fold line.

MAKING UP THE COLLAR

1 Press the embroidery carefully, face down, over a padded surface.

2 Pin the embroidered and the plain collar piece together with right sides facing. Tack (baste) and stitch around the front and outer edges, taking 1cm ($\frac{3}{8}$ inch) seam allowance.

3 Clip off the corners to reduce bulk. Turn the collar right side out, ease it into shape and press. Tack (baste) the neck edges together.

4 Topstitch close to the seamed edges (optional). Fold 1cm ($\frac{3}{8}$ inch) along the neck edge to the inside; press.

5 From the same fabric, or from similar white fabric (starched first, in either case, to make it easier to handle), cut a bias strip for the neckband, 4cm ($1\frac{1}{2}$ inches) wide and the length of the neck edge plus 5cm (2 inches). For some back- or front-opening styles the neckband will need to end flush with the collar, but on a pullover, for example, the ends are useful in holding the collar together at the centre front. The strip should be cut at a 45-degree angle to the straight grain and should be, if possible, in one piece, not joined.

6 Fold in 5mm ($\frac{1}{4}$ inch) along both edges of the neckband and press. Then fold the band down the centre and press again (see the diagram bottom left).

7 Slip the neckband over the raw neck edges with the ends extending evenly. If the collar is to open at the back, reverse the neckband as shown in the diagram top left. Tack (baste) the neckband in place, then stitch close to the folded edges and across the ends.

8 To attach the collar, catch-stitch the neckband just inside the garment neck edge, overlapping the ends and sewing them together.

The petals are worked in satin stitch across a single detached chain stitch (twisted twice), the stems in stem stitch, the buds in satin stitch and the leaves in buttonhole stitch.

▶ To adapt the collar for a back opening, eliminate the fold line and re-shape the edge with a curve (as here) or points.

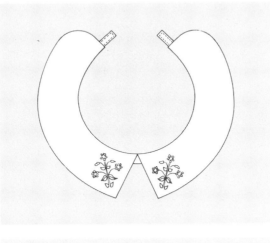

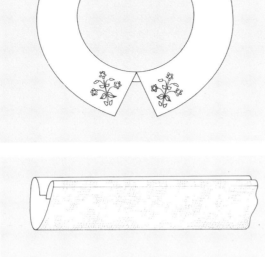

▶ To make the neckband, cut a strip of fabric at a 45° angle to the straight grain and 4cm ($1\frac{1}{2}$ inches) wide. Fold in 5mm ($\frac{1}{4}$ inch) on both edges and then fold in half down the centre.

THE HERB GARDEN

My very first garden consisted only of herbs. I grew them on the balcony of my flat and on the windowsill – at first simply to give flavour to my cooking, later for their decorative qualities. Then, when I acquired a proper garden of my own, there seemed to be so much to learn that I didn't know where to begin. My children were small, and I had hardly any spare time; and so I decided to make a virtue of limitation and continue to restrict myself to herbs. For the first couple of years, I was very strict, and only culinary herbs were allowed in. I turned down all offers of cuttings and seedlings unless I could cook with the plants, and soon I had so many herbs that there was no room – even if I had allowed it – for anything so frivolous as a hardy annual.

Lavender was the first exception to my rule; but even this plant – which I have loved since childhood – is a herb, albeit medicinal rather than culinary. Once I had broken my own rule, honeysuckle was hard to resist, and from there buddleia was but a step away. Other scented plants followed, and as I read more on gardening, I realized that the definition of a herb is much wider than I had first believed. It is a huge category, and includes all the most worthwhile plants, among them many with medicinal properties which are now being discovered.

I now have a much more eclectic approach to gardening, but I still think it's a good idea, if you have a small garden, to discriminate positively in favour of plants that have more to offer than just pretty flowers. I also think it's wise, if you can manage it tactfully, to turn down offers of plants unless you really want them in your garden. A garden should be personal to you and express your own tastes.

A personal embroidery

The same quality of personal taste and expression should also be found, I think, in an embroidered sampler. The sampler shown here is one of the most satisfying things I have done. It contains references to everything I enjoy about gardening – the colours and textures in my garden, the wildlife, the weather, and the different forms of plants, with their botanical names, historical significance, decorative aspects, scents and uses. I hope that my sampler will inspire you to make one of your own, including your favourite plants and appropriate proverbs and bits of poetry and song.

(One thing I learned, while making the sampler, is the importance of using even-weave fabric for any project including counted-thread stitches. The fabric I used was not truly evenweave, and this caused me many problems when taking a stitch from a vertical to a horizontal direction, or vice versa, and trying to keep it even.)

Three of the ideas contained in this sampler served as the basis for the projects given

Herbs were the first plants I grew and are still favourites. The projects in this chapter are based on this sampler, which reflects my feelings about gardens and the plants in them.

in this chapter: the line from the song *Scarborough Fair*, the myrtle garland and the potpourri.

Parsley, sage . . .

The four herbs featured on the tablecloth shown on page 127 are among the most commonly used in cooking. If you wish to grow them in your garden, you will find that although they all like chalk and good drainage, they vary somewhat in their other needs. Sage likes rich soil and moisture, and so does parsley – even more so; whereas thyme and rosemary prefer poor, dry soil. They all like full sun, although parsley tolerates some shade. Rosemary is hardier than rumour has it; wet at the roots does more harm than cold alone, so give it a sheltered position and be generous with grit when preparing the soil.

Just as fresh herbs make a significant difference to one's cooking and are well worth the care spent in growing them, so traditional table linen is well worth the care it requires. In our busy daily lives, most of us opt for the convenience of plastic or easily washable table coverings. Precisely for this reason, hand embroidered table linen makes the most of a special occasion or adds pleasure to a simple meal.

The herb tablecloth would be ideal for lunch with a friend, using a small round or square table. Or it could be used as a centrepiece, placed over a larger plain white or green tablecloth. Alternatively, you could use it as the top cloth on a circular occasional table with a long skirt – perhaps adding a jug or vase of the herbs for extra decoration.

Myrtle

I am lucky to live in a part of England where myrtle can be grown outside, with winter protection. In colder climates, it must be kept in a pot and brought inside during the winter. It likes conditions similar to those that suit all the aromatic Mediterranean herbs, but it cannot be kept quite so parched; otherwise the elegant glossy leaves will become dull.

There are several varieties of myrtle from which to choose. *Myrtus communis* is available in a variegated form; *Myrtus nummularia* creeps and is hardier than average; and *Myrtus tarentina* is a charming miniature version which, because of its size, is the easiest to grow in a pot.

The plant is appealing in any season. It seems never to go through the untidy stage common to most evergreens, and the fragrance of the crushed leaves is enticing; but when in flower it's irresistible. Towards the end of a good summer you will see the translucent neat berries and the rose-tinted buds alongside the full-blown flowers – and what flowers! Each flower has a disproportionately generous bunch of yellow-tipped stamens spilling from its centre, so that every individual bloom looks like a tiny wedding

Hyssop is an ancient and versatile plant, with pink, white or blue flowers. Bees love it and it distracts cabbage white butterflies from green vegetables. It has many herbal uses. Rock hyssop is a blue-flowered dwarf form which is more robust and longer flowering.

A traditional herb garden is a delight to cultivate. An endless variety of tones and textures, combined with its rich fragrance, make it a pleasure to work in and to walk through. Herb motifs are especially appropriate for embroidery on place mats and napkins. Each, for example, could display a different culinary herb.

bouquet. This fits in nicely with myrtle's bridal associations – it pre-dates orange blossom as an adornment for brides and wedding guests alike. For the guests a sprig of myrtle tied with white ribbon is traditional, but I have used this to decorate a handkerchief for a bride. Here the motif is worked on a blue background, to provide the 'something blue' of the traditional rhyme. If you prefer, you could work it entirely in white.

Potpourri

Making potpourri is one way of bringing the herb garden indoors for the winter; and for me the richly faded colours are as consoling as the scents. Displaying the dried leaves and petals in a favourite bowl on a mat such as the one shown makes them look even prettier. People often like to stir up the bowl of potpourri with their fingers, and the spilt bits will blend in with the stitched potpourri leaves on the mat and not look so messy. The mat will also help to protect the surface of the furniture; and because it is interlined (partly to help conceal the network of threads), it can also be used under a vase of cut flowers, where moisture is a potential problem.

In making your own potpourri mat, you need not use the colours shown here. You might choose a darker fabric or select threads matching the colours of your favourite potpourri mixture.

Parsley, Sage, Rosemary and Thyme

Four familiar herbs – used in the refrain of the song Scarborough Fair *– adorn this linen tablecloth. The individual herbs could also be used as motifs to decorate a set of matching table napkins.*

PREPARING THE FABRIC

1 Prepare the fabric (see page 139), and make sure that the grain is straight. Trim it, if necessary, to make a square measuring 5cm (2 inches) more, in both directions, than the desired finished size.

2 Mark the centre of the fabric, vertically, horizontally and diagonally. To do this, fold it down the centre in one direction, then work a line of tacking (basting) stitches along a central thread. Work another line perpendicular to this, to mark the centre point. Then work two diagonal lines between the corners (it will be necessary to press the fold lightly to obtain a straight line to follow).

3 Hem the edges of the square. To obtain neat creases, withdraw a thread 5mm ($\frac{1}{4}$ inch) from each

MATERIALS

80cm ($\frac{7}{8}$ yard) of evenweave linen, at least 80cm (31 inches) wide; the fabric can be fine or coarse, but it must be closely woven to prevent the embroidery threads from showing on the right side.

DMC no. 5 perlé cotton, I skein each of the following colours: 632, 904, 905, 906, 907, 987

DMC stranded cotton (floss), I skein each of the following colours: 632, 904, 906

Danish Flower Thread (or other matt-finish thread), I skein each of the following colours: 40 (light leaf green), 99 (pale mint green) and 302 (sage green)

Sewing thread to match fabric
Fine and medium-sized crewel needles
Medium-sized tapestry needle
Piece of cardboard (a cereal packet serves nicely), at least 20cm (8 inches) square.
Tissue paper
Tracing paper
Water-erasable pen

Size of finished tablecloth: approximately 74cm (29 inches) square.

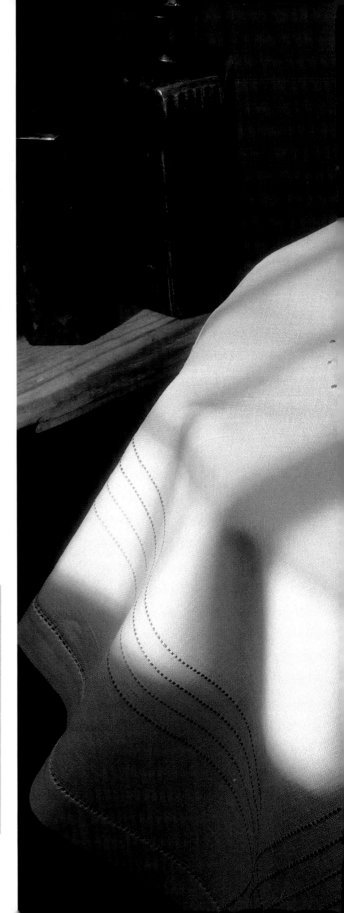

Trace the design for each herb, including the segment of the circle shown with the parsley (actual size). Tack (baste) the tracing of parsley to the line of tacking (basting) on the fabric and position the other tracings in accordance with it.

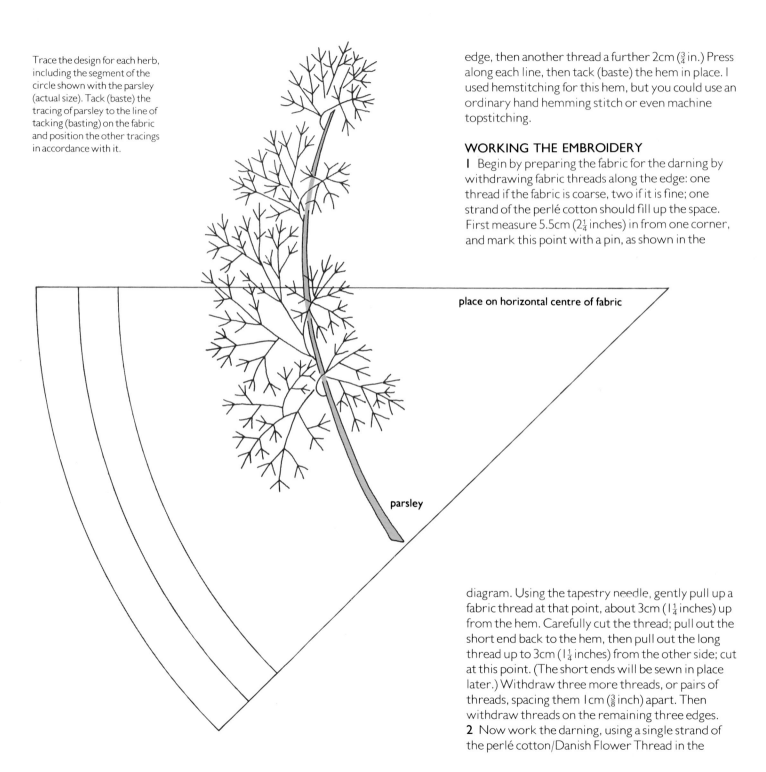

place on horizontal centre of fabric

parsley

edge, then another thread a further 2cm (¾ in.) Press along each line, then tack (baste) the hem in place. I used hemstitching for this hem, but you could use an ordinary hand hemming stitch or even machine topstitching.

WORKING THE EMBROIDERY

1 Begin by preparing the fabric for the darning by withdrawing fabric threads along the edge: one thread if the fabric is coarse, two if it is fine; one strand of the perlé cotton should fill up the space. First measure 5.5cm (2¼ inches) in from one corner, and mark this point with a pin, as shown in the diagram. Using the tapestry needle, gently pull up a fabric thread at that point, about 3cm (1¼ inches) up from the hem. Carefully cut the thread; pull out the short end back to the hem, then pull out the long thread up to 3cm (1¼ inches) from the other side; cut at this point. (The short ends will be sewn in place later.) Withdraw three more threads, or pairs of threads, spacing them 1cm (⅜ inch) apart. Then withdraw threads on the remaining three edges.

2 Now work the darning, using a single strand of the perlé cotton/Danish Flower Thread in the

sage

rosemary

thyme

following colours (beginning with the outermost line and working inwards): 906, 302 (sage green), 904 and 987. Do not knot the thread, but leave a short length at the beginning and end. Work over and under 2 fabric threads (or one thread if the fabric is coarse). When all the darning is complete, check the tension by pulling the fabric gently. Trim the ends to 3cm (1¼ inches), then, using sewing thread to match the fabric, oversew the short embroidery and fabric thread ends to the wrong side of the work, directly under the darning; take care that these stitches do not go through to the right side.

3 Work seeding stitches in each corner, using one of the four threads used for the darning (a different colour for each corner) and scattering the stitches randomly (see the photograph).

4 In order to work the centre motif, you must frame up the fabric. If you are using a slate frame, roll up the fabric edges and sew them to the edges of the frame; do not pull tightly, and take care not to make holes in the fabric. Alternatively, you can use a large ring frame, at least 35cm (14 inches) in diameter.

Measure up from the corner to prepare the fabric for the darning, as described in steps 1 and 2 on page 128.

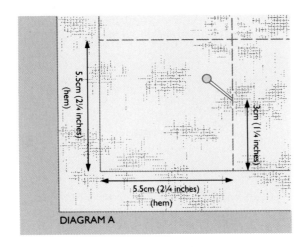

5.5cm (2¼ inches) (hem)

3cm (1¼ inches)

5.5cm (2¼ inches) (hem)

DIAGRAM A

5 Trace the design for each of the herbs onto tissue paper; include the segment of the circle given with the parsley as a guide for positioning.

6 Tack (baste) the parsley motif to the fabric, aligning the segment as shown on the page, so that the parsley crosses the horizontal line of tacking (basting). Tack the remaining motifs to the fabric, positioning them as shown in the photograph, the same distance from the centre point.

7 Parsley (The motifs can be worked in any order you like.) The parsley is worked mainly in shade 906, in perlé and stranded floss. Begin by working the main stalk, through the tracing, using stem stitch and one strand of perlé. For the main side stems, work single lines of split stitch. For progressively finer stems, use 2 strands of the floss in stem stitch, then one strand, in short straight stitches. When the network of branching stalks is complete, carefully tear away the paper.

8 For the parsley leaves, work fly stitches randomly over the stalks using the perlé (mainly 906 but with a few in the darker 905 towards the base of the stalk and some in the lighter 907 towards the top). The stitches should be very small – about 3–4mm (less than ¼ inch) in length – and should fan outwards (that is, with the tail of the stitch nearer the stalk).

9 Sage I chose Danish Flower Thread for the sage leaves because of its appropriate matt texture. Begin by working the leaves that have a central vein, using fishbone stitch and one strand of 302 and working

through the tissue. Outline the other leaves in stem stitch, still using 302. Outline the stems in stem stitch, using a single strand of shade 632 floss. Carefully tear away the tissue.

10 Fill in the stems using stem stitch and the outlined leaves with split stitch, using the same colours as for the outlines.

11 Rosemary Working through the tissue, first work the solid, dark leaves in 2 strands of the 904 floss, using stem stitch and two or more rows, as required. Next, work the leaves shown in outline only. Begin with the pale centres, using a doubled strand of Danish Flower Thread, shade 99 (pale mint green). Work in split stitch, bringing the needle up between the two strands and so producing the effect of a narrow chain stitch. Next, outline the leaf in stem stitch, using a single strand of 904 floss. Work up one side; then, at the top, work 3 or 4 short stitches above the pale stitches; then work in stem stitch down the other side.

12 Outline the main stem in a single strand of Danish Flower Thread, shade 40 (light leaf green), using split stitch. Pull away the paper, and fill in the stem with more rows of split stitch.

13 Thyme Work the entire motif through the tracing. Using one strand of perlé, shade 632, and stem stitch, work the main stem. Work the side stems in the same stitch and colour, but using 2 strands of floss. For the leaves, use a single strand of perlé, shade 987, and work individual chain stitches; lengthen the tying stitch slightly to form a stalk. When all the stitching has been completed, carefully tear away the paper.

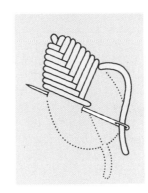

Fishbone stitch Begin with a short vertical stitch at the point of the leaf; then work diagonal stitches on alternate sides, overlapping them along the central vein as shown.

The lines of darning must not be pulled too tight or the fabric will be pulled into an uneven shape. To complete the edging, work seeding stitches at random in the corners.

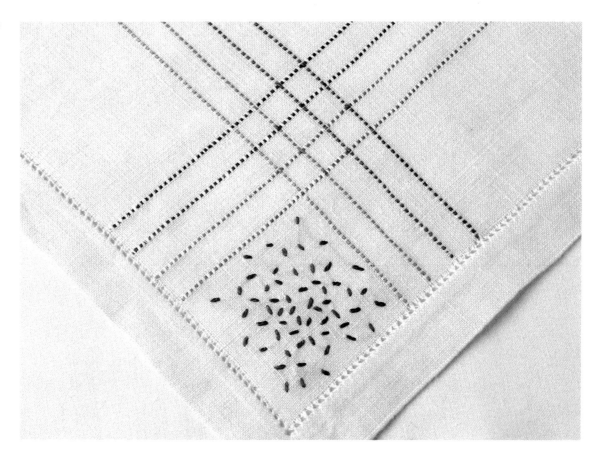

14 Borders To mark in the circular borders, first make a template from the piece of cardboard. Trace the segment given onto tracing paper, including the three outer lines. Cut out the tracing and draw around it on the cardboard. Trim along the middle arc and mark this, then trim and mark along the inner arc. Cut the segment out of the cardboard, cutting up to the inner arc only.

15 Position the cardboard template on the fabric, aligning the edges with two lines of tacking (basting). Draw along the curved edge with the water-erasable pen. Repeat, moving the template around the circle, until the inner border is complete.

16 Cut the template along the next arc, and use this edge to mark the next circle on the fabric. Repeat to mark the outer circle.

17 To work the inner border, first work French knots in a single strand of the perlé, shade 906, wrapping the thread once around the needle. Space the knots about 1cm ($\frac{3}{8}$ inch) apart. Fill in the spaces with more French knots, worked in shades 904, 987 and 302 (sage green Flower Thread).

18 Work the middle border of French knots, using the same four colours, but leaving a space of about 1cm ($\frac{3}{8}$ inch) between the groups. (You may wish to mark intervals of 2cm [$\frac{3}{4}$ inch] around the circle as a guide.) Place the darker colours, 987 and 904, on the outside of each group.

19 Finally, work the outer ring, which consists of individual French knots, worked in shade 904 and placed 2cm ($\frac{3}{4}$ inch) apart.

20 Remove the work from the frame. Wash it gently; iron it while still damp, working from the wrong side, over a thick pad.

Bride's Handkerchief

A sprig of myrtle, a traditional wedding decoration, is embroidered on this blue linen handkerchief, which will be a charming memento of the big day.

PREPARING THE FABRIC

1 Prepare the fabric as appropriate (see page 139). Turn under 1 cm ($\frac{3}{8}$ inch) on all four edges, and zigzag stitch this hem in place.

2 Mount the fabric on a rectangular frame, not too tautly. Alternatively, mount it in a ring frame.

3 Trace the design onto tissue paper, omitting the stamens, but including the corner mark.

4 Tack (baste) the tracing to the fabric, positioning the corner mark about 3cm (1$\frac{1}{4}$ inch) in from one corner.

WORKING THE EMBROIDERY

Use one strand of thread throughout. Begin by working through the tracing.

1 Starting from the bottom, work one side of the stem in shade 221. Work in stem stitch until the last centimetre (half inch), then change to split stitch. Continuing in split stitch, work the flower stems. (Note that this thread is dark and will show through unless you conceal it by running it under the stitches.) While working the top four stems, also outline the top four flower buds in the same thread, in tiny backstitches.

2 Outline the calices of the two lower pairs of buds, using shade 3346 and split stitch. (The calyx is the green cup-shaped support of the flower.) Outline the petals of the lowest two buds in white; those of the next two in shade 3687, still using split stitch.

3 Mark the topmost five leaves with tiny straight stitches, using shade 3345. Using the same shade, outline the other leaves, and mark their centre veins in small running stitches.

4 Outline the flowers in white, in small split stitches.

5 Outline the ribbon in longer split stitches, using shade 746. Tear away the tissue paper.

6 Thicken the main stem by adding a second row of stem stitch in 221, tapering it into the first row just past the bottom pair of buds.

7 Still using 221, work the top four buds in satin stitch. Work the next two buds in satin stitch, shade 3687. Work the lowest two in satin stitch in white near the top and shade 3687 nearer the base. The remaining parts of the design are filled in using the same colour as for their respective outlines or marking stitches.

8 For the top five leaves, work individual chain stitches. For the calices, use satin stitch.

9 Work the remaining leaves in fishbone stitch (see diagram, page 130).

10 Fill in the petals with rows of tiny split stitches, following the shape of the outlines.

11 Fill in the ribbon with longer split stitches.

12 For working the stamens, you may wish to make another tracing, including the stamens themselves and the petals, as a guide to positioning. Alternatively, you can work them more freely, using the trace pattern simply as a guide. First work the stamens in straight stitches, using one strand of the white machine embroidery thread; then tip each one with a French knot, in the yellow thread. Add

MATERIALS

Piece of blue handkerchief linen 38cm (15 inches) square

DMC stranded cotton (floss), 1 skein each of the following colours: 221, 746, 3345, 3346, 3687 and white

Very fine, glossy thread, such as machine embroidery thread, in pale yellow and white

Sewing thread to match fabric

Crewel needle, size 9

Tissue paper

Size of finished handkerchief: approximately 30cm (12 inches) square.

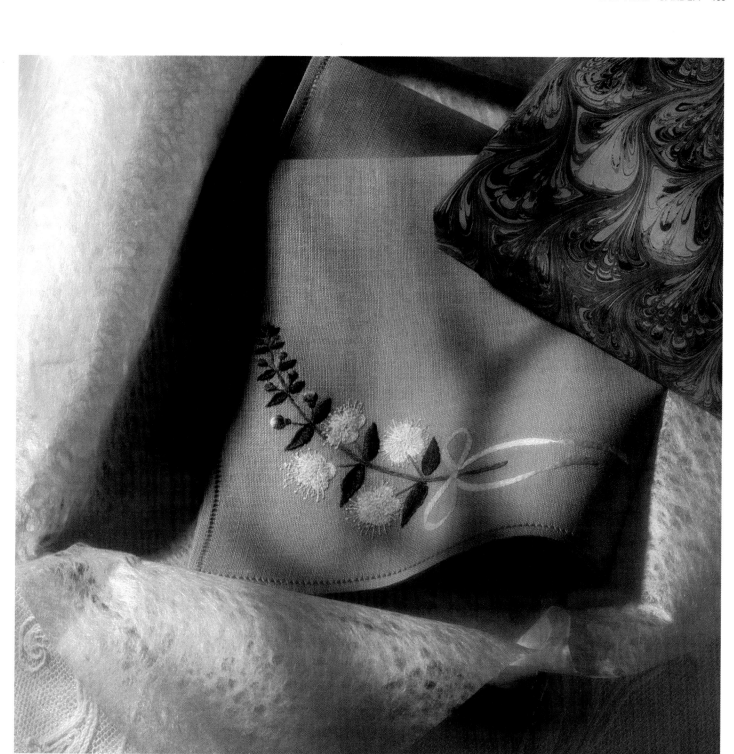

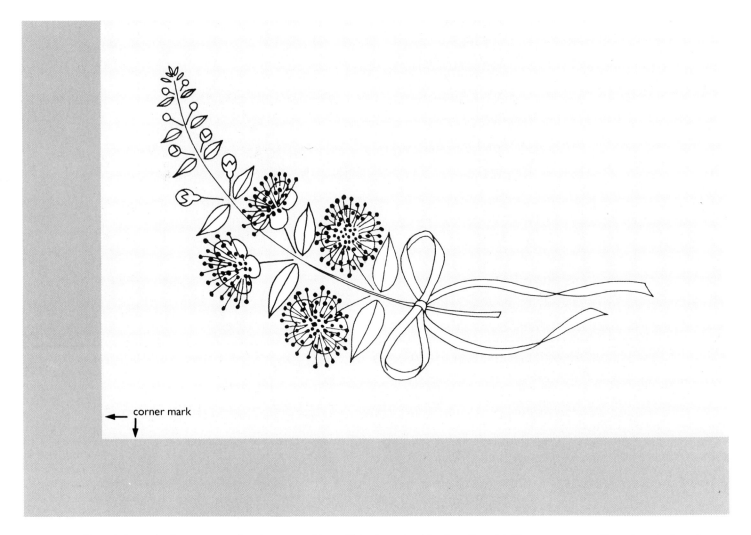

corner mark

some more French knots in the centre, using them to anchor the straight stitches where necessary.

FINISHING

1 Remove the embroidery from the frame. Trim it to measure 31.5cm (12½ inches) by first pulling a thread all around and then cutting along it.
2 Turn under a small double hem and sew it in place. You can use either ordinary hand hemming stitch or hem-stitching, as I have done here. Whichever you choose, be very neat – it makes all the difference.

Note: This charming blue handkerchief is a particularly delightful way of fulfilling the bride's traditional requirement for 'Something old, something new, something borrowed, something blue'. Furthermore, myrtle, once sacred to Venus, the goddess of love, is an especially appropriate symbol.

Trace the sprig of myrtle (actual size), omitting the stamens, but including the corner mark. Tack (baste) the tracing to the fabric, positioning the corner mark about 3cm (1¼ inches) in from one corner.

POTPOURRI MAT

Scattered straight stitches, chain stitches and French knots on this mat suggest the dried petals, leaves and flower heads of a traditional potpourri mixture. The mat is slightly padded to give a little extra protection to furniture.

PREPARING THE FABRIC

1 Prepare the fabric as appropriate (see page 139). Cut two pieces of the main fabric, at least 30cm (12 inches) square, and one piece, the same size, of the interfacing.

2 Trace the design given on page 136, repeating it three times and joining it at the centre to make the complete design. Transfer the design onto one of the main fabric pieces, using either a transfer pencil or dressmaker's carbon paper.

3 Tack (baste) the marked fabric to the interfacing around the edges of the design. Mount the two layers of fabric on a rectangular or slate frame.

WORKING THE EMBROIDERY

1 Using the colours listed below (or your own choice of colours), work the scattered stitches. I used straight stitches, detached chain and French knots. The variety of size and texture results from the different kinds of thread used (I used 2 strands of the floss). Scatter the colours and stitches as randomly as possible, using the detail photograph as a guide.

2 When the random stitching is complete, pin and tack (baste) the remaining piece of fabric to the underside of the work, through the centre in both directions and just outside the scalloped edge, taking care to keep it as smooth as possible.

3 Using a single strand of the coton à broder, shade 604, work the inner circle in backstitch.

4 Work the outer circle in chain stitch, using the same thread.

5 Work buttonhole stitch around the scalloped edges, taking care to keep the stitches as neat as possible.

6 Remove the work from the frame. Wash it gently, adding fabric conditioner, if necessary, and press it while still damp, from the wrong side, over a thick folded towel.

7 Using very sharp embroidery scissors, carefully cut around the scalloped edges, making sure not to cut through the stitches.

Note: Pot pourri can be made from almost any scented flowers, but rose petals and lavender buds are most frequently used because they retain their fragrance. There is a wider choice of aromatic leaves, such as scented geraniums, basil, woodruff, eau-de-cologne mint and bergamot. Bright flowers like calendula and borage add colour, spices, such as cinnamon and allspice, enhance the fragrance and orris root is used as a fixative.

MATERIALS

40cm (⅜ yard) of medium-weight cream-coloured linen or cotton, at least 61cm (24 inches) wide

Piece of medium or heavy sew-in interfacing 30cm (12 inches) square

A selection of embroidery threads; for the mat shown, I have used the following:

DMC no. 5 perlé cotton, I skein each of the following colours: 223, 740, 791, 963, 3350

DMC soft (matte) embroidery cotton, I skein each of the following colours: 2209, 2524, 2727

DMC coton à broder, I skein each of the following colours: 604, 3347

DMC stranded cotton (floss), I skein of shade 333

Medium-sized crewel needles

Embroidery transfer pencil or dressmaker's carbon paper (see page 140)

Tracing paper

Make four tracings of the
design, joining them at the
centre to make the complete
shape (actual size). Transfer
the design onto one of the
main fabric pieces.

MATERIALS AND TECHNIQUES

MATERIALS FOR EMBROIDERY

Most of the fabrics used in this book are of the type known as evenweave. They have a plain or common weave in which warp and weft follow the simplest possible over-and-under pattern. In the case of evenweave, the number of threads per centimetre or inch is the same in both directions. This kind of fabric is specifically intended for counted-thread embroidery.

In addition to the normal evenweave, in which single threads intersect, there is also hardanger (used especially for the Norwegian counted-thread work of that name), in which the weave is formed of double threads, and Aida cloth, a coarser fabric woven from groups of threads, normally 11 groups to 2.5cm (1 inch).

Single-thread evenweave is generally available in weights from 14 to 36 threads per 2.5cm (1 inch), although fine handkerchief linen, with more than 50 threads to 2.5cm (1 inch) can be obtained from some suppliers. Evenweave is normally made of cotton or linen (both of which are used for the projects in this book) and also, less commonly, in wool and in natural-synthetic blends. Although white and cream are the most often-used colours, many other shades can be obtained from specialist needlework shops and mail order suppliers.

For surface stitchery another useful fabric is calico (unbleached muslin), which can, if desired, be bleached. This provides a good, closely woven foundation for detailed work, and, being flat and inexpensive, is especially good for items in which most of the area will be covered with stitching.

Furnishing sateen, most often used to line curtains, is another good fabric for surface stitchery and for quilted items. It has a soft sheen and comes in a good range of colours.

As you gain experience in embroidery you will learn to recognize many other fabrics that are suitable for different techniques and purposes. Keep your eye open in dressmaking and furniture fabric departments.

Threads come in a variety of thicknesses, types and colours. For most of the projects in this book, cotton threads are used.

Stranded embroidery cotton (floss) is a lustrous, six-strand thread which can easily be divided into the required number of strands. Different shades can be combined in the needle for subtle shading.

Coton à broder, also called *brilliant embroidery cotton*, is a firmly spun, single strand thread with a slight sheen.

Perlé cotton, also called *coton perlé* and *pearl cotton*, is another glossy cotton thread. It has a distinctive two-ply twist, which gives it a beaded appearance, and comes in several weights, the commonest being nos. 3 (the coarsest), 5 (the most readily available and offering the greatest range of colours) and 8.

Soft (matte) embroidery cotton is a relatively thick thread with a matt finish.

Danish Flower Thread is a fine, slightly lustrous cotton thread which comes in an attractive range of natural-dye colours.

Linen embroidery thread is another fine thread with a slight sheen, available from specialist suppliers.

Crewel yarn is a wool thread useful where a soft, slightly fuzzy texture is required. The French Medicis wool has a more uniform thickness than English crewel wool, which makes it better suited to detailed work.

Needles For most surface stitchery a sharp-pointed needle with a relatively large eye is used. Crewel needles are best suited for fine work; chenille needles (which have relatively larger eyes and come in larger sizes), for thicker threads. For counted thread work a tapestry needle is used. This type of needle has a blunt point, which slips between the fabric threads without splitting them; it comes in a wide range of sizes.

Wadding (batting) is available in a variety of types and thicknesses. Today the most commonly used – and most widely available – wadding is made of polyester. Cotton wadding (often including a little polyester for stability) can also be found, especially in the United States. In Britain, polyester wadding can be purchased in 2oz, 4oz and 8oz weights, from quite thin to very thick. The 4oz weight is generally preferred for most purposes. In the United States, thinner, denser wadding is preferred, because it is generally used for quilts worked in running stitch. American wadding, or batting, is categorized by such terms as 'low loft', 'high loft' and 'extra loft', the latter being slightly thinner and denser than British 4oz. For extra thickness, two layers of wadding can be used.

Interfacing Several of the projects in this book call for iron-on interfacing. This comes in a variety of weights, suitable for different weights of fabric. Although woven iron-on interfacing is available, the most convenient kind for most purposes is the non-woven, since pieces can be cut economically, without reference to a grain.

Bonding materials For bonding two layers of fabric together, you can use either transfer or ordinary fusing web. The former, which has a paper backing and is sold in Britain under the trade name Bondaweb, has recently become available in the United States, where it is sold as Wonder-Under (by Pellon). The plain fusing web is available in Britain only in strip form (Wunda Web) for use in hems; in the

United States it is made by several manufacturers and comes also in large pieces. Both types achieve the same results; however, the transfer web is a little easier to use. The motif is drawn onto the paper backing (reversed, if it is asymmetrical) and is then cut out, slightly outside the drawn outline, and ironed onto the wrong side of the fabric. (Alternatively, the motif can be traced directly onto the web, on the adhesive side.) It is then cut out accurately, through the fused layers; the backing is peeled off; and the shape is then fused to the other fabric, which can then be trimmed to shape if required.

With the ordinary web, both web and fabric must be cut separately and positioned very carefully in order to ensure that none of the web sticks out around the edges. To avert this, pin the three layers in place and fuse them at several points with the tip of the iron. Remove the pins and press to fuse completely, covering the work with a cloth.

PREPARING THE FABRIC

Before using any fabric one or more preparatory steps are usually required.

Pre-shrinking *Always* pre-shrink the fabric if the finished item is to be washable; otherwise, all your painstaking work may be ruined. To pre-shrink the fabric, simply place it in a basin of hand-hot water, and leave it there for 15–20 minutes. Gently squeeze out the excess water, and place the fabric over a drying rack, keeping it as well supported as possible. Press it while it is still damp.

Starching If you are transferring the design by means of an embroidery transfer pencil, you will find that the marks will be easier to remove later if the fabric is first immersed in a fairly strong solution of laundry starch. This will also often make a small piece of flimsy fabric stiff enough to work in the hand.

Straightening the fabric Often fabric will be pulled off-grain in the course of being wound onto the bolt. You can discover whether this has happened by trimming the crosswise edges along a thread and then checking the corners with a set square (right-angled triangle) or some other square-cornered object. If the fabric corners are not 90 degrees to

Threads: (left) coton perlé 5; coton perlé 3; Danish Flower Thread; (right) stranded embroidery cotton; Marlitt viscose; coton á broder; crewel wool; (centre) perlé cotton.
Fabrics: (back to front) hardanger; calico; evenweave (35 threads); evenweave (28 threads).

each other, gently pull the fabric diagonally until it is properly square.

ENLARGING A DESIGN

Some of the designs in this book need to be enlarged to a given size before they can be transferred to the fabric. This can be done easily and inexpensively by many photocopying services. However, if you do not have access to such a service, you can enlarge the design manually using this traditional method. You will need a piece of tracing paper slightly larger than the printed design, another sheet of paper slightly larger than the full-sized design a pen, a pencil, a ruler and a set square (right-angled triangle).

1 On the smaller piece of paper, draw a rectangle the size of the original design. Using the ruler and set square (triangle) to ensure straight, perpendicular lines, divide the rectangle in two, vertically and horizontally. Divide each of these sections in two again. You will now have a grid containing 16 equal sections. If the design is very complex, you may wish to add more subdivisions.

2 On the larger piece of paper draw another rectangle of the specified size. For example, if

the design is to be enlarged to twice its size, and the original measures 20 by 30cm (8 by 12 inches), the second rectangle will measure 40 by 60cm (16 by 24 inches). Divide this rectangle in the same way into the same number of sections. Number the squares on both grids vertically and horizontally.

3 Tape the tracing over the design and copy the design square by square onto the enlarged grid (fig. 1).

This method can be adapted to enlarge (or reduce) any design to any chosen size.

1 Make the tracing paper grid for the original, as in Step 1, above. Then on the larger piece of paper, draw a horizontal and a vertical line, along the lower and left-hand edges. Measure off the chosen height or width of the finished design (whichever is the more important).

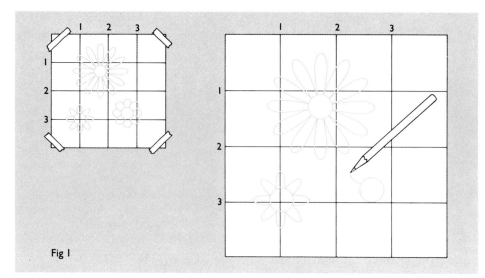

Fig I

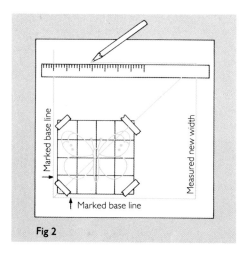

Fig 2

2 Tape the original grid to the lower left-hand corner. Draw a diagonal line from the lower left-hand corner through the upper right-hand corner of the original, past the marked height or width measurement. Draw a vertical (or horizontal) line from that measurement to the diagonal.

3 Complete the rectangle by drawing a line from the upper right-hand corner to the un-measured horizontal (or vertical) side. You now have a rectangle of the same proportions as the original but of the desired size (fig. 2). Divide it into a grid and copy the design.

TRANSFERRING THE DESIGNS

Dressmaker's carbon Special carbon paper, suitable for marking fabric, can be purchased in haberdashery (notions) departments. Place the fabric on a firm surface; place the carbon paper, coloured side down, over it; position the design on top, securing it with pins or tape. Go over the lines firmly with a ball-point pen.

Embroidery transfer pencil Unless the design has already been reversed when printed (or you wish to reverse it), you will need first to make a tracing of it, using an ordinary pen or pencil. Then turn the tracing over, and go over the lines with the transfer pencil. Position the tracing on the fabric, secure it at the corners, and press with a hot iron for a few seconds. Reposition the iron as necessary, without sliding it.

Tracing directly onto fabric If the material is not too thick, or large and unwieldy, or the design too complex, it is possible to trace the design through the material. First make a tracing of the design, then go over the lines with a thick felt-tip pen. Tape the tracing to a window with sunlight coming through it. Then tape the fabric on top, and trace with an ordinary pencil or water-erasable pen.

Working over a tracing Small, detailed motifs are often best worked over a tracing. Trace the motif onto tissue paper or thin tracing paper, using a hard pencil. Tack (baste) it to the fabric, then work the embroidery through both layers. When the work is complete, carefully tear away the tracing paper.

Prick and pounce transfer method This is a very accurate method and useful for transferring intricate designs. It is also well suited to designs that need to be repeated.

1 First make a tracing of the design, using good-quality, fairly stiff tracing paper.

2 Turn the tracing over and place it on a folded turkish towel. Prick holes along all the lines, using a large, sharp-pointed needle. The holes should be about 1cm ($\frac{1}{2}$ inch) apart.

3 Position the tracing, right side up, on the fabric. Using a small pad of felt, rub 'pounce' powder (which can be either powdered chalk or talcum powder, mixed – if necessary for contrast – with a little powdered charcoal) through the holes.

4 Carefully remove the tracing. A pattern of tiny dots will be left on the fabric. Join these up, using a water-erasable pen.

USING A FRAME

Most embroidery is best worked on a frame, although it is possible to work some small pieces in the hand, especially if the fabric has been stiffened.

A frame puts the fabric under tension, so that there is no danger of pulling the stitches too tightly and thus puckering up the work. It will also (if the fabric is mounted correctly) keep the warp and weft at right angles.

The correct degree of tension in the fabric will depend somewhat on the type of work being done and the purpose of the finished embroidery. A picture or sampler, when complete, will probably be laced tightly over board or card, so in the embroidery frame it can be laced tight as a drum. By contrast, an embroidered piece of clothing or cushion cover will be under little or no tension, so if the fabric is stretched too vigorously in the frame, the finished work may be distorted.

Types of frame There are several different types of frame, each available in a range of sizes. As you gain more experience and attempt different types of work, you will probably acquire several frames.

Ring frame This kind of frame is useful mainly for very small items, such as handkerchiefs, and for very large items, such as tablecloths, which are too large and unwieldy for even the largest adjustable frame.

If the fabric is delicate, it is advisable to protect it by binding the inner ring with ribbon seam binding or other woven tape (this also helps the ring to grip firmly) and by placing tissue paper over the fabric when mounting it in the frame. The tissue is then torn away, apart from that between fabric and outer ring (fig. 3).

1 To mount the fabric, first adjust the screw on the outer ring so that the two rings fit together smoothly but not tightly. Place the inner ring on a flat surface and lay the fabric on top, making sure that the grain is straight.
2 Press the outer ring over the fabric as evenly as possible, using the heels of your hands. The fabric should be quite taut (although in some cases a slightly slack tension may be desirable).

If the fabric is too loose, remove the outer ring, adjust the screw and try again; do not simply tighten the screw with the fabric still in position.

Fixed rectangular frame This can be an old picture frame, a homemade frame made from four lengths of wood or from artists' canvas stretchers. The fabric is mounted on the

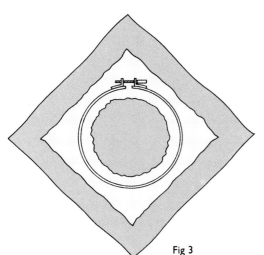

Fig 3

Lacing the fabric to a rectangular frame

frame wih drawing pins (thumbtacks), working outwards from the vertical and horizontal centres alternately. Although useful for some kinds of surface embroidery, this kind is not so satisfactory for work that involves counting threads.

Adjustable rectangular frame This type of frame, often called a scroll frame, consists of two horizontal rollers separated by two vertical laths. The rollers can be fixed at different distances, and fabric longer than the greatest distance can be rolled around them and unrolled as required; however, the maximum width of fabric is determined by the length of the rollers.

1 Neaten the edges of the fabric. This can be done by turning them under and hemming with one or two rows of machine zigzag stitch or by stitching woven tape or seam binding over the edges. For a very firm side edge, place a length of cord at the edge, then fold the fabric around it to form a casing, and stitch to hold the cord in place. The lacing (step 5) is then worked through the casing.
2 Find the vertical centre of the fabric, and tack (baste) along a thread to the opposite side; repeat along the horizontal centre.
3 Pin the lower edge of the fabric to the strip of webbing on one roller, matching the fabric centre with the centre point of the webbing (previously marked). Oversew the fabric to the webbing as shown. Repeat on the upper edge of the fabric.

4 Position the rollers on the laths so that the fabric is held fairly taut.
5 Using cord or strong thread, such as linen carpet thread, in a large needle, lace the sides of the fabric to the sides of the frame as shown. Cut the thread about five times as long as the sides of the fabric, and knot the starting end securely around the upper crossing points of the frame. When both sides have been laced, pull the cord all along the length to make the fabric as taut as possible, then tie the ends securely. Or, if a slightly slack tension is required, relax the lacing threads slightly before knotting; this tends to give more satisfactory results than simply leaving the tension slack to start with. Check that the lines of tacking (basting) are straight and at right angles to each other.

FINISHING

When the embroidery is completed, the work will usually benefit from a wash. This can be done while the work is still in the frame. Use a detergent you trust, and dilute a small amount of it with lukewarm water. Make sure to dissolve it thoroughly if it is a powder. Place the framed fabric in the bathtub, and apply the detergent solution with a sponge, rubbing *very gently*. If you have a shower attachment, use this to rinse the work thoroughly; otherwise, use a jug of water. When the work has been well rinsed, leave it to dry in the frame.

Embroidery that has been worked in a ring frame or in the hand will usually need pressing. Place the work face down on a thick pad made from folded sheets (not turkish towels, which might leave an imprint), and press carefully with a steam iron or a dry iron over a damp cloth.

MAKING UP A CUSHION COVER

It is a simple matter to make up a plain cushion cover without a zip fastener. Simply trim the embroidery to measure 2cm (¾ inch) larger than the finished cover on all sides, and cut another piece of fabric, for the back, the same size. Place the two pieces together, with right sides facing, and tack (baste) and stitch them together 2cm (¾ inch) from the edge, leaving a gap large enough for inserting the cushion pad (pillow form) in one side. Cut across the seam allowance at the corners to reduce bulk (oversew these edges if the fabric frays easily), press the seam open, and turn the cover right side out. Insert the cushion pad, then slipstitch the opening.

Inserting a zip fastener It is easiest to insert a zip fastener that is at least 5cm (2 inches) shorter than the length of the seam.

1 Place the front and back of the cover together with right sides facing, and stitch them together along the edge in which the zip is to be inserted, changing to the longest machine stitch where the zip teeth will be positioned. Press the seam open.

2 Place the zip face down, centred, over the seam, with the zip pull tab extended. Tack (baste) it in place close to the teeth.

3 Stitch along both sides and across the lower end, either by machine, using a zipper foot, or by hand. Pull the tab down slightly and stitch across the top.

4 Open the zip. Stitch the remaining seams of the cover as described above.

LACING OVER CARD
Embroidered pictures are often prepared for framing by first being laced over a piece of thick card (mat board). Allowance must be made for this when cutting out the fabric; a margin of 3–5cm (1¼ inches) should be left on all edges. If you have not allowed enough fabric, you can stitch the work to another piece of fabric, using a closed zigzag (or satin) stitch in a contrasting colour.

1 Cut the card to the desired size of the finished picture (adding a little extra if necessary to allow for the inner edge of the frame).

2 Place the embroidery face down, and centre the card on top of it. Fold the two longer sides over the card, and hold them in place temporarily with masking tape.

3 Unwind some strong thread from the reel (spool), but don't cut it off. Thread it through a needle. Beginning at the centre, and unwinding more thread as required, work herringbone stitch through the two edges as shown (fig. 4), out to one side. The stitches

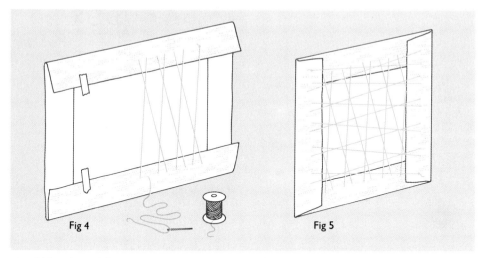

Fig 4

Fig 5

should be about 1.5cm (½ inch) apart. Fasten off the thread.

4 Measure off a length of thread slightly longer than that already used. Cut it off, thread it through the needle, and work from the centre to the other end. Before fastening off, pull the stitches along the entire distance to make sure the thread is taut. Also check the embroidery to see that it is still correctly positioned. Fasten off.

5 Fold over the remaining edges and lace them together in the same way (fig. 5).

MAKING A TWISTED CORD
The number of strands required for a twisted cord will depend on the desired thickness of the cord and on the thickness of the threads used. Sometimes, as in the projects in this book, the number of strands will be specified. You can get an idea of the finished size by twisting a few strands tightly together; the cord will be about twice as thick.

1 Cut the strands 3 times the required finished length. Tie one end of the strands around a doorknob or drawer pull, and tie the other end around a pencil.

2 Holding the free end, turn the pencil around and around until the strands are tightly twisted – so tightly that they will kink up if the tension is relaxed.

3 Bring the two ends together and tie them in a knot. The already-twisted strands will

twist around each other. Shake them to even out the twists, and knot the folded end. Trim both ends and fluff out the strands.

To attach the cord to a cushion, place it on the seam, and sew it by hand, working back and forth just under the cord, with each stitch picking up a few fabric threads and the underside of the cord (fig. 6).

Where the ends meet, overlap them slightly, and wind thread firmly around each end, above the knots. Trim off the excess, and insert the ends in a small gap left in the seam. Sew the edges of the gap together neatly, anchoring the ends of the cord securely at the same time.

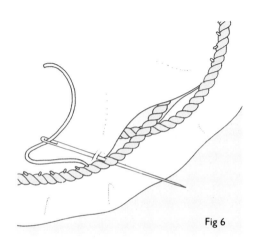

Fig 6

$\mathcal{I}$NDEX